This book © Just Press Books 2022
(justpressbooks@gmail.com)

Luther Blissett

POSTCARDS FROM THE SWAMP

Tales of horror and decadence from Venice Biennale

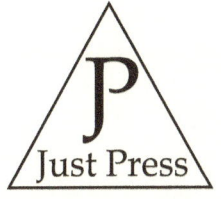
Just Press

CONTENTS

Foreword..7
Chapter 1: The heart of the matter......................11
Chapter 2: We're only in it for the money............83
Chapter 3: The greatest show on earth................143
Afterword..203
Acknowledgments.......................................205
Notes..207

Foreword

Venice Biennale's first edition was held in 1895, long before E. H. Gombrich published "The Story of Art" or the BBC broadcast John Berger's "Ways of Seeing". It was there before the MoMA was even conceived of, one century before the Tate Modern opened its doors to the public. Art Basel's senior by 75 years and 60 years older than documenta, Venice Biennale started decades before the world of contemporary art became a self-sustaining industry and turned into the hydra-headed monster that it is today. It came into life when nobody could imagine that all sorts of artworks would enter into the cycle of mass visual consumption which is a by-product of the compulsive consumerism that regulates the life and death of all goods sold in supermarkets around the planet. Certainly back then nobody could foresee the marriage of art and entertainment, or rather predict that the former's fate was to become a subsidiary of the latter. No one thought that an art exhibition could have the potentiality to attract people with no art education or even, as is the case of many visitors of the Biennale, no interest whatsoever in art. In 1895 the intensive programs of art marketing borrowed from corporate propaganda, the gentle enforcement of mass participation, and the tight control of all men's and women's free time had yet to be applied on a large scale and still less in a field, the art world, that was still uncharted territory for commoners. It was absolutely impossible to foretell the huge economic and social proportions that any art related event, including the Biennale itself, could take in the late 20th Century. It all started long before any effort was made to engage everybody in contemporary art and to eventually turn individuals into a mass of consumers, albeit only visually and distractedly, of paintings, sculptures, photographs, installations, and videos that very seldom make any sense in their ordinary lives.

For many years now I have worked at the Biennale. Not 'for' the Foundation which is headquartered at Ca' Giustinian near Piazza San Marco and that organizes the exhibition, manages the Central pavilion in the Giardini and the Italian pavilion in the Arsenale, wages the communication campaign, sells the tickets, and runs almost everything except the national pavilions, the bookshops, and the collateral events (both official and unofficial). Actually, I worked for it, but just for a couple of weeks in 2008. Apart from that, I have always worked 'at' the Biennale, that is the exhibition itself. I have been employed in the bookshops, in some collateral events, and most of the time in a national pavilion in the Giardini as an exhibition attendant, which is one of the least exciting positions that the art world can offer. I have worked for curators, artists, museums, temporary work agencies. I have worked part-time and full-time. Alone and in team. I have mounted and dismantled installations, packed artworks, mopped the floor, sold catalogues, fixed minor damages, ordered catering services, given information, scolded impolite visitors, organized shipments, supervised renovation works, assisted press professionals, attended to bureaucratic stuff. During both the International Art Exhibition and the International Architecture Exhibition. Until 2022 they used to last about six months, but then the duration of the 59th Art Biennale was extended to seven months. Yet, more important is the fact that they alternate each other, so that every year there is a Biennale. There are also an International Theatre Festival, an International Festival of Contemporary Dance, an International Festival of Contemporary Music, and the renowned Venice International Film Festival. But they are a different story, since they last just a few days and do not offer so many job opportunities. In fact that is what the Biennale means to me: having a job to make ends meet. I did not study art or architecture and do not have any particular interest in neither of them. I just happen not to be able to find a decent regular job. So, for the time being I am stuck at the Biennale. I have had breaks doing other temporary jobs, but they never turned out to be the turning point that I have been waiting for since I graduated. For me, as for many of my generation, Venice is still the swamp that it was before the beginning of its reclamation in the 5th Century: a place where life is arduous and finding an employment is as difficult as walking with one's feet buried in sludge. It is a demanding city and, strange as it may seem, at times working at the Biennale can be a hard occupation.

Since 1995 I have gone through 17 editions of the Biennale, most of them presided by Paolo Baratta - the man that was considered to be so successful in his job that in 2015 the Foundation's statute was altered in order to allow him to serve a fourth term as its President. I have met many people from all over the world and seen many things. I came to realize that the art world is not as hunky-dory as it might appear if observed by an outsider. In this book, which could easily have been one thousand pages long, I try to tell what is often untold, unseen, unsuspected, or even purposefully hidden. It ranges from the utterly comic to the horrific, from the depressingly dismal to the obscenely outraging, from the insulting to the abominably disgusting, from the personal to the collective. Usually the official version of any event is written by its makers, those who have the power of speech and the privilege to be listened to; those who are trusted by whom is accustomed to being instructed from above and to receiving information that has already been processed for them. The narrative about the Biennale is no exception. I think it is high time to tell the rest of the story, to complete the picture by relating what happens behind the scenes, how the people who work there are treated, what its visitors are really like, what part greed has in it. Here I offer an account of the most famous contemporary art exhibition from my perspective, that of a disenchanted underdog of the world of contemporary art that has grown tired of listening to a story which very often falls short of relating the facts as they really are.

Chapter 1: The heart of the matter

In 1895 and for almost one hundred years afterwards, Venice Biennale was a melting pot for the high society, an occasion for the artists to exhibit their works in one of the world's most beautiful cities - visited by all sorts of intellectuals, royal families, financiers, magnates, potentates, bon vivants, and any other subset of the human species that could afford a stay in Venice when it was not yet a destination for cheap tourism. Thus, it comes as no surprise that the art exhibition soon became the most famous and coveted international cultural event. Not simply an illustrious forerunner but the originator of a formula to clone even in its recurrence. So, most of the major art festivals that have sprung since the second half of the last century are held every two years and therefore are called 'biennale'. The website of the Biennial Foundation, which does not have anything to do with Venice Biennale, lists hundreds of art festivals that take place every two years, while the International Biennial Association lists more than fifty members. However, the only one that immediately comes to mind when the word 'biennale' is used with no further specification is still the one which emerged from the greenish waters of Venice and speaks

Italian: *la Biennale*.

After all, there is no other event that can claim to have survived two world wars (during which it was suspended), a shift from monarchy to Fascism and then to a lame democracy, innumerable economic crises, the social revolutions of the 60's, the political turmoils of the 70's, and the steamrolling course of globalization without losing a jot of its appeal. In 2020 the Architecture Biennale was cancelled due to the Covid-19 pandemic, but when it was held the following year it came back in full swing and the attendance figures were beyond all expectations. To make a list of all the masters and art celebrities that have participated in the 58 editions of the art Biennale is almost beyond imagination. Their names are written in bold letters in every book on the history of art. One could pick up a random volume from the shelves of the modern and contemporary art section of any library, flip through its pages and be sure to spot dozens of artists that exhibited at the Biennale. The ambition of all artists and curators is to have their names printed on the pages of the thick, expensive catalogue that every two years bears the promise of immortality and, hopefully, of an increase in quotations. What matters is being there, rubbing elbows with those who made history and the few ones that make money. So, it happens that the official logo of the Biennale, which can be used by the national pavilions of the Giardini and the Arsenale and some of the minuscule stars of the galaxy of collateral events orbiting in town, is craved like an amulet that can boost one's career or at least help securing a grant. Be it fame, greed, or an honest urge to contribute to the never-ending discourse on contemporary art, everybody has their own good reason for wanting to be at the Biennale, even if just at its periphery. But artists and curators are not alone in wanting to have a piece of the action. Nowadays a whole army of the most disparate (and sometimes desperate) individuals want to make an appearance on stage, albeit for only the blink of an eye. And, if short it must be, what moment could be better than the glittering days of the exhibition's opening?

If the weather does not play tricks, the days between the end of March and early June are the perfect time to visit Venice. It is quite warm but not as hot yet as in summer, so one can stroll along the canals or get lost in the maze of narrow alleys that crisscross the city in every direction. Many have observed that the city's shape looks like a fish swimming to the West, but all the *calli* ('streets') that traverse its body make it look like a deformed brain or a dysfunctional intestine congested with foreign bodies it is unable to expel. Tourists can stroll for hours, walking on streets that have never felt the pressure of a car tire. When weary, they can sit by an old well or find some rest inside a church. There they can relax in silence on a wooden pew and enjoy the shade and the peace, or scan the paintings that adorn the walls and altar, perhaps finding out that they were made by the same artists whose name they came upon in an old, battered book on the history of art. But in such spring days (usually on the second week of May, in late April in 2022), in the very same town there is a small but combative army of people who cannot find rest and do not have time for the Tiepolo's or the Tintoretto's. Where they want to go there is no such thing as calm, because they head right where the madding crowd is gathered. It is a small area cut off from the rest of the city by an invisible fence raised more with the intent to buttress the self-importance of whoever happens to be inside rather than to keep out those who do not have an official invitation. Where they want to be - some for professional reasons, others for pure fun - is the area of the Giardini, the public park at the far eastern end of Venice in which the oldest and most important pavilions of the Biennale were built. The Central pavilion (once the Italian pavilion, which was relocated to the Arsenale in 2007) and those of France, the USA, Germany, Great Britain, Spain, the Netherlands, Belgium, Japan, Russia, Canada, Australia, and other nations are all there, amounting altogether to a total of 31 pavilions. They are buildings of the most diverse styles and shapes that every two years, for about half of the year, are supposed to host the best living artists of every single country. So, during the vernissage all sorts of notables and wannabes join artists and curators to cross the thresholds of the pavilions as if they were believers led by bishops through the portals of St. Mark's Basilica in Christmas. The parallel is quite apt, since the rite that is being celebrated has been the same for aeons and will always be the same, like a comedy that keeps on being staged in the same theatre from time immemorial with no alterations apart from (some of) the actors. So, during the official reception of every pavilion all artists, curators, ministers of culture, donors, and whoever has gained the right or the privilege to ascend the altar of institutional loquacity recite the very same lines that have already been uttered on thousands of similar occasions. Sometimes what they say does make sense, although one could play a tape of a speech given ten years before and nobody would notice any incongruity. No matter what they say, the people in front of them listen like faithful churchgoers aware that only after a boring flow of sermons they will be rewarded with what they have been awaiting for so long. They know that after fifteen, thirty or, in the worst case scenario, forty minutes of liturgical garrulousness, when all the big wigs will have had their turn to vent their admiration, appreciation, gratitude, only at the end of this tunnel of words there will be a comforting light. Finally communion will be administered to the congregation in the form of free drinks handed out by indifferent waiters or disconcerted museum interns lured to Venice with the promise to serve the cause (not the cocktails) of contemporary art.

If there is one situation that stands as an irrefutable proof that modern humans still belong in the kingdom animalia, that situation is an open bar. It has the power to trigger a repressed ferocity and make bodies clash against one another as in a movie about the sinking of the Titanic directed by David Cronenberg. An open bar is a battlefield where "civilisation appears as a very thin film below which the old demons are crouched, waiting for the opportune moment to reappear and suffocate precariously civilised men in ceremonies of pure instinct and irrationality"[1]. One can see middle-aged women wrapped up in Chanel clothes crying for not being able to get hold of a flûte of prosecco, students trying to sneak behind the bartenders to snatch a bottle of beer, stupefied attractive young girls lulling their empty glasses like insane mothers trying to revive their dead babies, grown up men gurgling alcohol as desperately as a London's real estate agent that at 5pm on Friday rushes to a pub in Chelsea trying to postpone for as long as possible the moment when he will have to go back home and spend the evening with his family. Yet, the real function of that alcohol boiling in cheap plastic cups smeared with lipstick and lousy snacks' grease is not only to help people get tipsy. Every single drop flowing down their throats has the power to lift them to a higher level of petty self-aggrandizement. In fact, for them it bears witness to a privilege. It is proof of their belonging to an international elite of art connoisseurs that have the entitlement to show up at the Biennale's vernissage. Obviously this is just a mass delusion, considering that the roughly 30% of participants who really have a good reason to be there do not want to mix up with the remaining 70% of parvenus that successfully begged for an invitation or managed to jump the fence behind the German and the British pavilions or to sneak in from the embankment behind the Austrian one. Most of the crowd at the vernissage consists of fakes, posers, illusionists that lose control of their acts and end up embarrassing themselves chasing a dead rabbit that will not come out of their hat. People who affirm to be rich, educated, of noble lineage, extraordinarily popular in their countries, advisors to the most wealthy art collectors, publishers of books that only circulate in masonic underground art circles, scholars of whatever discipline can conjugate a random humanistic branch of knowledge with economics, appointed directors of museums that will be built in the future if funds will somehow be allocated by a yet-to-be-informed ministry of culture, owners of the yachts moored almost in front of the main gates of the Giardini, journalists who contribute without being paid - although they are clearly in need of money - to art blogs whose only raison d'être is to apply worldwide for press credentials, relatives of deceased artists, fiancés (that is to say sugar-daddies) of the above mentioned stupefied attractive young girls. A collective comedy of make-believe in which everybody is, in their own eyes, the lead singer of the choir.

Perhaps the saddest characters of the three days of openings and celebrations are the students and the interns that come to the Biennale full of expectations like the would-be stars that go to Hollywood to start a career in the movies but end up shooting porn. Some of them look like they have spent all their lives in anticipation of the Biennale, eager to take part in an event they suppose to be plentiful in job opportunities. They waste their time awaiting the chance to meet someone that might change their lives offering them an employment, a grant, a residency, perhaps just an occasional assignment to pass off as a freelance collaboration. Their dreams are soon shattered, because in a world of pretence nobody has much to offer them except promises that will never become facts. Their journey to the promised land turns into a shabby vacation to Venice spent grabbing free tote bags and imploring to be admitted to the night parties that for a few days lighten up a city that usually plunges into darkness shortly after sunset, all the blinds of its old palaces closed shut at 8pm.

It goes without saying that alcohol is never enough. Nothing is ever enough during the *vernice* ('vernissage').

Press kits, USB sticks, canvas bags, complimentary catalogues, brochures, leaflets, t-shirts, pins, posters, all imaginable gadgets disappear as soon as they are taken out of the cardboard boxes that are stored in every room and corner not already occupied by an artwork. So many parcels are delivered to the Giardini the days before the official opening of the Biennale that one could use them to make a life-size replica of China's Great Wall - an overdue gesture of gratitude towards the People's Republic of China for having bought cash in hand half of the bars and restaurants in Venice. If they are not very expensive, the goodies inside the boxes are given away as the food distributed to the homeless outside supermarkets on Christmas' eve. Usually anyone grabs more freebies than they can carry around, care to keep, or manage to tuck into a Ryanair-approved hand-luggage. So, the most lousy giveaways brought from all over the world are abandoned on the tables used for the catering services or on the benches lined along the main promenade of the Giardini. Since sooner or later USB sticks and bags can come handy, the predestined casualty is the information material printed on paper - because it can be easily retrieved in the internet and, above all, because almost nobody is keen on spending time reading press releases and curators' introductions while all around there are so many events going on. This does not mean that there are not serious journalists or scholars that try to focus on the artworks and that in order to do so go through all the available information to gain an insight that later on they will transmit to their readers and students. But unfortunately they become invisible among the multitude of people who only have hands to grab but lack eyes and ears to understand. Those who are there with a real interest in what is exhibited amount to a fraction of participants that year after year seems to decrease and is sadly overwhelmed by the rapacious flock of predators in search of pure fun and fancy trophies who sometimes show no mercy even for the catalogues of the national pavilions. In fact, at the end of the day it happens to see official publications in pristine conditions, sometimes still wrapped in cellophane, lying on windowsills around town or on the seats of a *vaporetto* ('waterbus') like newborn babies left at the mercy of local passersby that will probably use them to fill in the bookshelves of the shabby apartments they rent to the very same people who abandoned them. Hours of work of artists, curators, photographers, designers forever trapped in pages that will never be read nor just simply flipped through, especially if the books are not good enough to be sold to second-hand bookstores or presented as gifts to friends that did not make it to the *vernice*. In truth, it must be said that many catalogues are not worth keeping. For the funds at the disposal of every national pavilion vary in quantity but are seldom proportionate to the costs of the original plan, so during the preparatory months many projects are progressively slimmed down until they are stripped to the bone. Apart from the obvious cost cutting on personnel's wages, the quality of the paper, of the ink, and of the binding of the catalogues is a likely victim for a sacrifice on the altar of budget. As a result, many lousy books that are paid for with the money coming from the pockets of unknowing tax-payers or wealthy patrons have as many chances of ending up in someone's private library as an outdated Ikea catalogue. Some curators try to cover the production costs with the aid of sponsors that would be much more happy if they could have their names on the uniforms of their local football team. I have seen catalogues in which so much space was allocated to the contributing companies and their logos that they might have been easily mistaken for an abridged version of the Yellow Pages. Sometimes quantity over quality is the ruling idea, thus too many copies of a book are printed and in the course of the Biennale their price is reduced to make them more palatable and, during the last weeks, they are handed out like Reichsmarks after WW2. Suffice it to say that as late as 2015 the Greek pavilion was still trying to get rid of the stacks of catalogues of the exhibition of Lucas Samaras that it hosted in 2009. Meant to be a gift for the most interested visitors, the book became a relic that year after year the exhibition attendants passed on to each other like a baton in a relay race with the instructions to put it in the hands of whoever happened to set foot inside the pavilion (I use the past tense but I would not be surprised to find out that some copies are still hidden in some dark recess of the building).

Money is always the main concern of artists, curators, and project managers. They nonetheless always manage to squander it at the speed of light. First of all, they do not seem to be able to calculate the ratio by which all costs rise as one crosses the bridge that connects Venice to the rest of the planet. Then, once in town, they seek the assistance of local craftsmen and professionals who eagerly accept to work for them for a reasonable compensation without making it clear that any fifteen minute intervention not mentioned in the contract will cost as much as a whole working day in any other Italian city. But this is not enough. If on one hand set-up costs are always underestimated and a multitude of unpredicted petty expenses haunts even the most accurate spending plan, on the other there is the awareness that the fleeting days of the vernissage have to be used to the full to liaise with as many people as possible. And that, too, can be quite expensive. Journalists must be convinced to include a particular exhibition in their top five list of the projects that make a visit to the Biennale worthwhile. Ministers of culture, chairmen of art foundations, sponsors, patrons need to be reassured that what they paid for has a slight chance to win the Golden Lion. Gallerists cannot be left alone, wondering whether they will really manage to make big money out of the artist they have supported for so many years and that they finally managed to squeeze into the Biennale. Brooding collectors must be inoculated with the conviction that the installation they are looking at is both the summa of all the art produced so far and a foregoer of anything that will be made in the future. Scholars, critics, museum directors have to be enlightened about the topical issues addressed by a supposedly groundbreaking exhibition everybody was unconsciously waiting for. Part of these tasks are performed by a press office unit that can be made up of anybody from an illiterate intern to four employees of one of the most expensive European communication agencies. The choice is between cheapness and professionalism, but the latter is not guaranteed even when an obscenely high slice of the budget is spent for the services of a topnotch press office. I had the chance to work side by side with the employees of one of the best British communication agencies. They did anything they could do to promote the exhibition during the vernissage and the following six months. They were so kind that they helped me clean the pavilion (one of them even cleaned the toilet), lift heavy weights, do any chore they were not expected to do. After the opening days every few weeks they sent reports with weblinks and PDF's of the press coverage of the show. They did an excellent job, precisely what they were paid for and even a bit more than what they were supposed to do. Not exactly the same could be said of the team of one of the biggest and most expensive French communication agencies that I had seen in operation a few years before. The chief was a woman of the uttermost impoliteness that used to pick her nose in public, while the good-looking girls working under her direction seemed to have been paid more to shake their bums on the face of the male attendees than to distribute information material. Obviously they disappeared right after the opening days, very probably without bothering to waste one single minute to promote the exhibition.

Very often the communication campaign is carried out by the curators or by the artists themselves. They have to sustain a tour de force that in the few days of the vernissage comprises any conceivable means to catch the attention and the endorsement of as many journalists and art professionals as possible. Personal relations must be lubricated in order to establish alliances, strengthen positions, dilate egos. Interviews and meetings are arranged in advance or on the spot and are held beside the artworks or under the shade of a tree in the Giardini.

Other locations chosen to pursue such strategy are restaurants' balconies, hotels' lounges, and any other place equipped with a barrier of exclusivity, visible or not, capable of fending off the assaults of those without enough affluence or influence to trade in for an admission to the private quarters of contemporary art. However, it is a good idea to display some consideration also for the 70% of the vernissage-goers that do not carry much weight because of their irrelevance on any account other than their function of lending their bodies to fill in the space left vacant by the 30% that are justifiably there. All in all the populace's support is always welcome. Although it cannot help win a Golden Lion, it contributes to build up a circumscribed, temporary popularity that allows the artist/curator combo to revel in the idea that what they present at the Biennale is art for the masses rather than a sophisticated branch of the entertainment industry. So, more money is spent to throw cocktail parties on privately rented islands or on tourist boats converted into floating dancehalls, in palaces uninhabited since the 18th Century or in deconsecrated churches, in semi-legal premises of dubious not-for-profit cultural associations or in school gyms. Almost any available corner in town is rented to offer a soiree fired with cheap booze and music played by dj's recruited among either the entourage of the curatorial team or the throng of local dj's unemployed for most part of the year. Thus, another slice of any given budget may be spent with a total disregard of the expenses that a pavilion might incur into in the six months during which it will be open to the general public.

The night parties are nothing more than extensions of

the inaugurations held in front of the pavilions during the day. The only difference is that, since there are more people than those who manage to sneak into the Giardini and the Arsenale during the day, the level of contemptibility is raised yet more. "For such is the nature of excited crowds (and every crowd is automatically self-exciting) and that where two or three thousand are gathered together, there is an absence not merely of deity but even of common humanity. The fact of being one of a multitude delivers a man from the consciousness of being an insulated self and carries him down into a less than personal realm, where there are no responsibilities, no right and wrong, no need for thought or judgment or discrimination - only a strong vague sense of togetherness, only a shared excitement, a collective alienation. And the alienation is at once more prolonged and less exhausting than that which follows self-poisoning by alcohol or morphine. Moreover, crowd delirium can be indulged in, not merely without a bad conscience, but actually, in many cases, with a positive glow of conscious virtue. For, far from condemning the practice of downward self-transcendence through herd-intoxication, the leaders of church and state have actively encouraged this kind of debauchery, whenever it could be used for the furtherance of their own ends"[2]. Moronic smiles cross the faces of totally uneducated students euphoric for having access to some free drinks while men double their age drool at the sight of the firm bodies of their young girlfriends. Would-be artists join in to have a look at what their lives might have been if only they had possessed the few mental gifts needed to get a diploma at the Accademia di Belle Arti. Old unsuccessful artists come to pour bile over the art system that never understood their talent, as do all the painters and sculptors that "Not being able | To create art | They will not | Understand art | They will consider their failure | As creators | Only as a failure | Of the world"[3]. Drinking as much as possible is the only tactics they can think of to get their due. Meanwhile all around them there is a throng of human beings not the least interested in what they are supposed to be celebrating, acting like mediocre imitators of the guests of Jay Gatsby who attended his parties even though they had never met or seen him.

During the Biennale the national pavilions inside the Giardini represent their countries as much as an embassy or a consulate. They do not bear the same importance for international relations as the diplomatic offices located in Rome, Milan, and other major Italian cities including Venice itself. Neither do they release passports or offer political asylum to art refugees. Nonetheless, for about half of the year they function as windows into the culture, the history, the values, and obviously the wealth of nations that never, apart from some rare exceptions (for instance Venezuela in 2014 and Australia and some other countries in 2021), renounce to exhibit the works of their most outstanding or promising artists and architects. So, it is only natural that during the vernissage a varying number of civil servants and state bureaucrats of both high and low ranks fly to Venice to keep an eye on how their countries are represented and, above all, on how state money is spent. Their fancier counterparts are the fashionable pen pushers working for the foundations appointed to manage some of the pavilions (as is the case, for example, of the Swiss and the Dutch ones). Usually they differ in appearance and manners, the latter looking like well paid museum interns (forgive the oxymoron) while many of the former are an upgrade of the traditional figure of an office clerk sprung from the imagination of Franz Kafka. What they share is the confidence to be the descendants of the Chinese Mandarins of the 7th Century, the civil servants that reached their position in the government apparatus after undergoing a system of examination designed to select the men most suitable to become the empire's white collars. So, a good portion of them tend to overestimate their job, their skills, their social position. Very often they think to be fit for more grandiose appointments and nurture the ambition of climbing the hierarchy of the institution they work for and going down in history as the man or the woman who managed to turn it into a more efficient organism. Certainly a few of them have the competence and the painstaking determination to pursue such a career. But there are many others who cannot be bothered with any activity other than shuffling papers day after day looking forward to the next payslip, probably the only document they take time to read twice. Small families of these office sloths are always attached to the official delegations visiting the Biennale, an effortless duty that they regard as an opportunity for a free trip to Venice. Although they fit perfectly in the environment of the Giardini and the Arsenale (Italy being the perfect habitat for slow, lazy mammals that make their lair in public offices), sometimes they manage to shock even the most experienced observers. They can be overwhelmingly surprising in their shabby attires, sporting filthy sneakers and shorts when they are expected to stand as an example of the impeccability of their own country's bureaucratic system. I remember one woman in particular. She worked for a not well specified department of a ministry that covered anything from tourism to art, education, and sport of a small North-European country. I saw her a few times, in different years. She looked like a tame clone of Edith Massey, John Waters' muse. Once she attended the vernissage wearing a blue chenille training suit. She looked like one of those creeps that end up being voted freak of the month on the websites that collect cctv frames of the weirdest humanity shopping at Walmart. She never failed to struck me for her total lack of any feminine quality and, it goes without saying, for her attitude of complete disregard for the Biennale, art in general, and, I presume, her own office. Her eyes were two perfectly horizontal lines. A couple of apertures squirting hatred at all living beings showing any sign of good humour or satisfaction with their current condition. Eyes that surely would have gained her a close-up shot in a western movie by Sergio Leone. She was one of the three most evil-eyed women that I have met at the Biennale. Yet, her feature which is still haunting my memory is a vivid image of her open mouth. More precisely, a clear picture of her teeth. In fact, the last time I saw her I had the misfortune to spot her in the crowd besieging a food table during an opening reception. Probably it was her second charge, since her teeth were already caked with something that had been food but was now just an undefinable mush drenched with alcoholic saliva. What appeared to be chunks of *tramezzino* (a sort of patty melt) or a pap of crisps and pastries plastered the gaps between her teeth and I wondered how long they would stay there. Perhaps just until the next gulp of warm, lousy prosecco would wash them down her throat, cleansing her mouth of the most disturbing evidence of her inadequacy of being there. Or maybe for as long as it would take her to pick every single lump of food with the tip of her tongue, secretely savouring again the endorphin-releasing taste of another working day spent as a vacation paid by the State. However it may have ended up, those food remains, turned pink thanks to her decomposing lipstick, made me think of blood-soaked raw meat stuck between the fangs of a wild animal. Indeed that woman was a perfect specimen of that not so small subclass of the human species that keeps encrusted in its DNA primitive instincts which give rise to behavior patterns that clash with the false idea still held by many that the world of contemporary art is populated by sophisticated philanthropists and creatures of superior intellect. Not only are people like that woman always prone on jumping on free food and drinks, they also show a hostile attitude whenever they spot any intruder violating the perimeter of their territory. They entrench behind their desks to defend their turf, guarding their jobs like wild animals protecting their cubs from the attacks of potential competitors, usually younger and more capable than them. They live in constant fear of losing their privileges to a species one step ahead of them along the path of professional evolution. They cling to their employments and the benefits they offer, gripped by the frightening knowledge that in a truly fair society it would take just a graduate of modest intelligence and erudition to threaten their office's status quo and snatch up their job. At the Biennale, to their dismay, they see hundreds of graduates and young professionals starving for an occupation. What they do not grasp is that there is no need to panic, for most of the people there are equipped with an intelligence and an erudition that often fall short of being modest. Including the majority of those who, if taken at the face-value of their collection of degrees, masters, internships, and all sorts of qualifications printed on paper, are presumed to be the ones that will bring about a radical change in the bureaucracy of the art world. Indeed, what that woman with food all over her teeth probably still does not imagine is that all grades of education and training in the fields of art management and preservation of cultural heritage are meant to instruct on how to keep the system running without major discrepancies with the past. So, her office and the whole system will not feel the urge to replace her until she retires. Any genuinely fresh idea might jeopardize the position of those who sit in the control room of the machine. Thus, to avoid any risk, the policy opted for everywhere - from a ministry of culture down to the most insignificant petty art foundation - seems to be always the same: to train and employ an army of yes-men that out of sheer laziness and personal convenience guarantee an unshakeable will to keep things, good and bad alike, exactly as they are. In so many years spent working here and there at the Biennale I have very seldom seen anyone take an unexpected decision. It looks like everybody is scared to displease someone else above them and fall from grace. Even the Foundation itself is a shelter of clusters of like-minded men and women that try to build up a secure environment ruled by conformity. In a city like Venice, where work opportunities are scarce, even the humblest job at Ca' Giustinian is a godsent gift. Therefore, nobody is willing to take the risk of doing the most insignificant thing that has not already been approved by the high ranks of the Foundation. For instance, it takes a solemn oath and an age-old personal acquaintance with the supervisors of the Giardini to have the permission to postpone for a few minutes the closing time of a pavilion or to do anything in the communal areas. During the Architecture Biennale of 2016 I spent the most part of an afternoon on the phone in order to have the authorization to place some chairs in the park to accommodate the participants in a workshop, but I was denied the permission to hang some A3 posters of the very same event. During the years my inquiries have been met with replies ranging from the obvious "pavilions are prohibited from doing this and that" or "all special events must be submitted to the approval of the Foundation" to the more Italian style ones like "send me an email", "phone Ca' Giustinian and ask there", "I don't want to be scolded by my chief", and "it's six o'clock, I'm off, do what you want, I don't wanna know" (my favourite). I must express my gratitude to all the supervisors who have turned a blind eye when I needed them to do so, but I keep on thinking that things should be made easier for everybody in spite of the old Italian belief that efficiency and accuracy stem from rigid bureaucracy.

The three days of the vernissage are the longest. They never finish at 7pm, which anyway is one hour later than the regular closing time for the general public. In the evening, when all the speeches have been delivered and all the appetites have been satisfied, minds and bodies leave the Giardini and the Arsenale and head towards the dinners and parties scattered in the six *sestieri* ('boroughs') of the city. Before the sun disappears behind the skyline of Porto Marghera (the industrial district built in front of Venice right after WW1) the open areas around the pavilions are left to the cares of the few persons charged with the task of returning them in pristine conditions for the following day. In the course of a few hours they dump tons of rubbish along the canal behind the British and the Australian pavilions, the latter a polished black cube that in the quietness of the late evening looks like a gigantic musical machine out of one of J.G. Ballard's early short stories. It seems to play one single inaudible note on which sooner or later everything going on at the Biennale is destined to attune to. Its undetectable sound is as monotonic and dull as are most of the people that not long before were roaming the Giardini and as will be the long days of the many people working there for the next months. As the sky turns from blue to red and then black, when all humans have left the area, rats are the only living beings with a superior intelligence that spend time around there ransacking the temporary rubbish dump. They scuttle among empty bottles and discarded press kits totally oblivious of the fact that not food, but rather glass, plastic, paper are the results of human waste that they can find in abundance. Totally unappealing to the hungry overproportionate rodents, heaps of bin bags and crates contain what remains of objects that were used for only a few minutes. Large quantities of disposable cutlery, packaging material, A4 sheets of paper, invitations printed on expensive cardboard, fliers, brochures, poor-quality catalogues, magazines, maps, programs, useless gadgets, folders, envelopes, and stationery of all sorts spend a night out waiting to be picked up by a trash-collecting boat and, hopefully, to be recycled. Perhaps the wheel of Samsara of inanimate things will spin one more time for them, giving them a new life under a new form. We consumers of the 3rd Millennium love recycling. It helps us feel less guilty and, more importantly, it is less bothersome than its more basic yet more advanced closest relative: reuse. Although the latter is surely more sensible and ecofriendly than recycling, it requires some annoying, time-absorbing operations such as cleaning and putting away that divert any household from more entertaining occupations. Laziness suggests to dump into the downcycling plants everything that is conveniently replaceable, although now we are all aware that in the long run such attitude will turn up to be less beneficial than reuse. In this regard the Biennale is no exception, so in the piles of rubbish raised behind the British and Australian pavilions during the vernissage one may happen to spot, for instance, good wine glasses thrown away just because nobody cares to wash and store them for future use (yet they are nothing compared to the tons of reusable material, especially wood and glass panels, that are dumped during the dismantling operations which take place after the end of the exhibition). In their enduring fragility they stand as symbols of the carelessness with which resources of all kinds are wasted. But they also provide a memento of how every individual's idea of self respect and his or her understanding of one's professional worthiness are liable to shift into an excessive sense of pride and, sometimes, sheer pretentiousness. Apart from some notable exceptions, most people hate to be seen washing the cutlery used for the opening reception or sweeping a floor littered with the dust and gravel brought into a pavilion by the thousands of feet coming and going all day long. Even the nerdiest interns have some concerns about busying themselves with humble tasks, especially if no office tools are required to do the job. At least a stapler or a printer can make one feel like they are handling important documents; but a broom or a dish sponge used in the darkest service rooms of a pavilion are dreaded like doomed objects that might cast a spell upon their bearers, condemning them to spend the rest of their working life as janitors of the very same art institutions they dream to direct. So, the widely shared attitude is to throw away as many things as possible and to hide the rest behind some door that hopefully nobody will open for a few years. This is why during the vernissage there are places in the pavilions and around the Giardini where one can see glasses, ice buckets, chairs, or tables jettisoned at sunset and left floating in time and space like unwanted ballast. And the more the sun goes down, the hastier are the operations of discard of all things which, although they might come handy the next year, are not necessary the following day. In fact, at around 7pm the body clocks' alarms of the people in the Giardini and in the Arsenale ring in unison and remind them that it is time to leave and make ready for the dinners and parties. Men and women abandon the areas driven by the hysteria-inducing urge to attend all the night events in Venice, not only because they are affected by what Aldous Huxley defined as the "disgusting vice of crowd-intoxication, of downward self-transcendence into subhumanity by the process of getting together in a mob"[4], but also because it is the best strategy they can think of lest they miss the party which the next day will be the most talked about. Whoever is in charge of an exhibition goes as far as double checking if all the artworks are still there and locking them safely inside the building that for about half a year will preserve them like a bank vault (which means totally unsafely). A fatal mixture of tiredness, hurry, and laziness makes the curatorial team quite confident that in due time the exhibition attendants and the personnel of the cleaning company will get rid of everything that must be disposed of, no matter how long it will take.

My personal experience provides a perfect example of such inclination towards waste and *scaricabarile* ('buck-passing'). One year the project manager of the show I worked for as an exhibition attendant was so kind as to invite me to join the artist and the curator for a cocktail party on the terrace of the Paradiso, the bar in front of the main gates of the Giardini. The only thing I should do before going, she said, was to rinse a few glasses used for the inaugural reception that had been held in front of the pavilion. No problem, I thought, since tidying up was one of the duties listed in my contract. I washed all the glasses that had been brought to a small room equipped with a water sink, including one that shattered in my hands slashing my right index finger. It left on it a v-shaped scar which is still there as a warning of the countless pitfalls lurking in the glittering world of contemporary art. When I was finished and about to leave the building with a gory strip of toilet paper rolled around my finger my phone rang. It was an employee of the Foundation, one of the many supervisors in charge of a set of not well defined logistical operations that include the maintenance of the pathways and of the communal green areas. She wanted to remind me that every pavilion must take care of the disposal of the rubbish it produces. I replied that I was aware of that and, anyway, we did not have much to dump. "ALSO THE TRASH THAT YOU PILED UP OUTSIDE THE PAVILION!", she added in capital letters. So I went out expecting to find a few plastic cups and the usual chipped flûte glasses. There was nothing in front of the main entrance, just some litter here and there. Not enough to justify a phone call from someone supposed to have more pressing issues to sort out. I decided to have a look around to make sure that the phone call was a purely gratuitous act of harassment aimed at stressing that in the months ahead there would be zero tolerance of public displays of disrespect for the sovereign authority of the Foundation. But as I turned around the corner of the pavilion my field of vision was slowly filled by a scene that my brain took some time to process. What confronted me was a jumbled configuration of shapes of different hues of brown, red, and green. Little by little my eyes managed to isolate the objects that apparently had been duplicated an incalculable number of times and arranged in such a way as to compose a scene of mind-bending lovecraftian chaos. Dirty bordeaux glasses, empty wine bottles, and the crates they were shipped in covered an area of about five square metres. Defying rationality and the law of gravity, the remains of the doubtlessly appreciated gift of one of the sponsors looked like props on the set of a disaster movie. Boxes and splinters of wood of any size, bottles whose labels had been torn off by raving nails, glasses abandoned everywhere in all but the upright position were sprinkled with morsels of food still bearing the marks of teeth interrupted in the midst of their dismembering operations. Everything was still wet with wine, smeared with oily fingerprints and marks left by lips unfit to speak. They were the last signs of human activity left by a debauched herd of human beings that had suddenly been hit by one more wave of overindulgence that washed them on the terrace of the Paradiso. Staring at the quantity of trash and dirty things they left behind I started to despair. Washing all the glasses which were not broken and subdividing the rubbish into piles of recyclable material would have taken hours of unpaid work. Moreover, after that I would have had to bring all the refuse to the garbage heaps along the canal behind the British and the Australian pavilions. Thinking about all this my feeling of discomfort grew into that kind of frustration which eventually leads to repressed rage. All I could do was phone the project manager and inform her of the situation and my inability to cope with it. "Don't worry", she said, "throw away the trash and put the glasses in our storehouse. Tomorrow I'll have someone wash them". I did so and then, too tired to engage in whatever social activity, I went home. It goes without saying that the following day nobody washed the glasses. They were left there to gather dust and tiny carcasses of drunk insects. Soon they were covered with a menacing looking, velvety green mold. So, when the vernissage was over and all except me left Venice to go back to their countries and jobs, I gave away a few glasses to an Australian boy who used to brew his own beer in his girlfriend's flat and threw away the rest. Each day I dumped a few of them after closing time. Like a petty criminal that has to make disappear the proofs of the illicit trades he finds himself involved in without knowing how or why. A task only fit for the least important member of the gang. The one that, if necessary, can be left behind.

What is not destroyed during the stampede of the vernissage is destined to suffer a slow but steady process of decay that takes place during the following months. The artworks are no exception. The unrelenting humidity of Venice and the clouds of dust that the centipedal public rises from the aisles and pathways of the Giardini and the Arsenale are the worst environmental conditions for an art exhibition. Even more so if one adds up the thousands of dirty fingers that, in spite of any invitation not to do so, any artwork is inevitably bound to attract. Saint Thomas nonchalantly sticking his fingers into Christ's wounds, as seen in so many European paintings of the past centuries, would be fit to fill in the position of patron saint of all those who can not trust the authenticity of a painting or a sculpture if they do not manage to peel off a small crust of colour or take away a sliver of stone. Perhaps Mark Rothko had such people in his mind when he wrote that "sensuality applies ultimately to our sense of touch, to the tactile, which, whether we want it to be or not, is still the final justification of our notions of reality. Our eyes, our ears - all of our senses - are simply the indications of the existence of a veritable reality that will ultimately resolve itself to our sense of touch"[5]. But also the immateriality of the video installations is not exempt from trouble: functioning at least eight hours per day, sooner or later the projectors' lamps blow up or their lenses need being refocused. A variety of small and big problems arise in the long weeks leading to the end of November, when the show ends and everything is shipped away or dumped. The pavilions themselves, solid looking as they are, show ever new marks of ageing left upon them by a sometimes harsh weather and an always insufficient care.

The lack of maintenance for the pavilions is especially manifest when it rains. Ceilings leak, sometimes dangerously close to the artworks and very often the most advanced technology devised to fix the problem is a plastic bucket positioned underneath the seepage (my personal record is seven buckets at a time). Even if the roofs are in perfect conditions, ponds of rainwater form here and there in the Giardini. They can be small or some square metres wide. Their depth varies from a few centimetres to one that might pose a serious threat to a Chihuahua dog bold enough to dare wade across them. The slope in front of the British pavilion makes water flow towards the turnstiles at the entrance, so when it rains heavily a brook of mud and gravel rushes in front of the Russian, Venezuelan, Swiss, Danish, and Nordic Countries posts. It can leave them unscathed or deposit a little rubbish and rubble in front of them, but it can happen that it finds its way into those that have been built below the pathway's level. In such a case the miserable exhibition attendants who work in the calamity stricken pavilions might have to engage in an epic struggle to prevent the natural element that most distinguishes Venice from penetrating from above their heads or under their feet. Meanwhile, wave after wave of undaunted visitors walk around wrapped up in nylon ponchos with an image of Rome's Colosseum on their back, yet another symbolic reminder of how unable or unwilling to fit into the context of the Biennale and of the entire city many tourists are. An astonishing amount of people seem comfortable in noisy plastic gaiters, some of which, now out of stock, used to be one of the funniest puns ever intended by the local shopkeepers. 'Gold' was written above the heel of the left one, and 'On' over the heel of the right one. So, very probably foreigners thought that they had 'gold on', that is to say a good pair of gaiters or just a pair of flimsy ones with a stupid name invented to make them look fancy. Probably no one among the people who purchased them was aware that in the local dialect the word *goldon* means 'scumbag' and that in today's street parlance it is used to describe an idiot or an easily gullible person.

It is a bit elaborate to take off a poncho or a pair of gaiters, and it is especially annoying when one knows that they must be put on again after a few minutes. So, exhibition attendants like me suffer in silence the noise made by human bodies wandering around wrapped in acres of coloured plastic. What I find more difficult to put up with is the fact that so many people are too scared that their five euros umbrellas might get pinched that they will not let go of them and leave them at the entrance. During the many years that I have worked at the Biennale no theft of an umbrella has ever been reported to my attention, but

I have seen people choose not to visit a pavilion when not allowed to carry their umbrellas with them and members of a family take turns to guard their umbrellas leaning against a wall by the entrance while the others attended the show. I have also been physically assaulted by a man who valued his umbrella above anything and anybody in the world and thought that leaving it in my care would have been like leaving a child in the hands of a paedophile. Therefore, in order to avoid arguments or just too tired to ask the same thing for the umpteenth time, at a certain hour I and many other exhibition attendants let people walk around the pavilion holding their umbrellas and wearing any sort of wet garment they are happy to sport. So, thousands of drops of water foil any attempt to keep the floor dry and the humidity under control. Every single one of them hits the floor making a sound that reverberates through the nervous system of the exhibition attendants, especially those that are not blessed with the faculty of calling upon a professional cleaning company to have the floor scrubbed, mopped, and dried up (I know of one exhibition attendant who had to work until 9pm - three hours after closing time - to clean his pavilion after a day of incessant rain).

Rainy days turn out to be the most depressing, annoying, and irritating for anybody working at the Biennale. Yet, at least being inside a pavilion means that one is sheltered from the wind gusts that strike the personnel by the turnstiles and at the exit. The gazebos that are supposed to shield them from the bad weather are not always sufficient to stop the rain that sometimes seems to come horizontally and they are definitely incapable of preventing the thick November humidity from soaking through their clothes and into their bones. There are days in which the mist surrounding Venice is so dense that if the tourists standing in Piazza San Marco raise their eyes to the sky they cannot see the pinnacole of the bell tower, which vanishes into a white fluff of suspended rain drops. It is in those days, spent in a cold gazebo turning down holders of expired passes and giving the same information over and over, that one most values the basic comforts that come with a decent job - such as a chair to sit on for half an hour in a dry tepid corner - or just the simple warmth of a cup of hot tea. A sense of hollowness fills in one's mind, while his or her body is exposed to wind, humidity, and low temperatures. In the course of time self-abandonment turns off the immune system in an unconscious attempt to commit suicide by abandoning oneself to a form of silent, gradual physical deterioration hastened by the forces of nature. So far there have not been reports of any such death, so it seems that all one can get is a flu or a soar throat, not enough to leave this world or to call in sick the next day. However, should one really have the firm intention to shuffle off the mortal coil of the Biennale, it might be a good idea to keep an eye on the weather forecast and hope for a gale or one of the summer tropical storms that, thanks to climate change, hit Venice with a destructive violence. In that case Mother Nature could unexpectedly put an end to someone's life in a matter of a few seconds. In fact, since they are located in an area that does not offer much protection against the winds blowing from all directions, the Giardini are occasionally swept by blasts of such violence that can wipe out anything standing in their way. Locals still remember the tragedy that happened in 1970, when a tornado hit Sant'Elena (Venice's most easterly point, right beside the Giardini) like a monstrous truck crashing at full speed on a quiet village road. It literally sucked up in the air a *vaporetto* full of commuters, making it fly like a pigeon feather caught in a whirlwind. Up in the sky went the boat, and then down it fell like a tailspinning plane out of control. It became a huge nail that under the hammer of its own weight pierced the brackish water of the lagoon. It reached for its miry bottom, polluted by the toxic particles that spread like a 20th Century black death through air and water from the industrial complex of Porto Marghera. All the people inside the waterbus died, and now in Sant'Elena there is a small unpretentious monument in their memory. Luckily similar events have not occurred ever since, but every time the weather gets too humid and windy the personnel that works outdoor can be seen stretching their necks nervously in the air to scan the sky. They are not trying to decipher the messages hidden in the steamy white lines sketched by the planes taking off from Venice's airport. That would be an act of modern divination that could only intensify their repressed urge to quit their job and take a vacation out of the most touristic city in the world. What they try to do by looking attentively at the heavens is to prevent being hit by a falling tree branch. Although so far there has not been any casualty, the frequency with which the ageing trees inside the Giardini loose pieces big and small makes any sensible being aware that the issue is not 'if' but rather 'when' someone's head will be the target of a wooden bomb. In case such concern seems too far fetched, suffice it to say that in 2015 a guard that was standing by the turnstiles was missed by a mere few centimetres by a free-falling branch that, if put vertically, would have looked like a small tree. Some metres in length and too many centimetres in diameter to be dismissed as a harmless broomstick, it fell at her feet with such violence that she had to leave her post and go home in a state of shock. That very same year another branch fell from a height of about six metres on the roof of a small cabin used to store the tools of the gardeners. It damaged it but fortunately it missed by a couple of metres a consistent number of visitors queuing at the toilets between the Dutch and the Belgian pavilions. The noise made by the wooden bolt breaking smaller branches in its free fall and finally crashing on the storehouse scared them but nobody seemed to be much affected by their brush with death. Perhaps they thought it was part of the fun. Two years later a couple of trees were knocked down by a storm and one of them fell a few metres away from a group of visitors sheltered in a kiosk. I took some pictures of it and noticed that inside it was as empty as a bamboo stick, so I wondered if that tree had suddenly succumbed to a parasite or if perhaps its roots had absorbed briny water seeped into the Giardini's terrain from the lagoon. What is certain is that its conditions had just been overlooked at the expense of the visitors' safety. The other tree collapsed on the Uruguayan pavilion damaging its roof, which took some weeks to be restored. And the same accident happened again in 2019, when because of a strong wind a tree fell on the pavilion of the Czech Republic and Slovakia, damaging its roof and leading to its temporary closure (at the time of writing this book the roof has not been repaired and the pavilion was not opened for the 2021 Architecture Biennale).

It was not a tropical storm but pure negligence that in 2011 almost caused the destruction of one of the most fragile pavilions in the Giardini. The Finnish pavilion, built in 1956 and designed by Alvar Aalto, is considered as a small national treasure by the Suomi people. Its blue and white colours are the same as those of the country's flag and it is made of one of the oldest building materials: wood. On its left side there is a gravel pathway leading to the Hungarian pavilion, while on the right one there is a small green area with a nice English-style patch of grass and some bushes and trees. In 2011 one of the trees there had a bifurcated trunk, one part leaning towards the windows of the bookshop inside the Central pavilion, the other towards Aalto's pavilion. One fine day the former collapsed and came off the main shaft of the tree without harming anybody or causing any considerable damage. Obviously what remained standing of the tree inspired a sense of lingering danger, particularly in the people who worked inside the Finnish pavilion. So they inquired of the firemen guarding the Giardini whether it was safe to keep it open to the public or if it was safer to close it until preemptive measures would be taken in order to avert any further fall. When they were told that the situation was under control and no other accident was to be expected, they went back to work as usual and kept on busying themselves with their daily routine. All went well for some time, until when what was far from being unpredictable and inevitable happened, fortunately without harming anybody. The remainder of the tree fell over Aalto's helpless, fragile shed. Most of the damages were suffered by the roof but, much to everybody's surprise, the building managed to bear the blow notwithstanding its old age. All in all it went well, so the issue was handed to the insurance companies of the Foundation and the municipality, which spent some time trying to cast the responsibility of the accident onto each other. Eventually the Finns received their compensation and took the chance to chip in some money out of their pockets to restore the whole pavilion. Nobody made a fuss about what happened, the local press did not bother to cover the event, and apparently any official complaint or excuse was kept at the level of the usual, formal exchange of letters.

All lovers of art and architecture should be contented that the story had a happy ending, yet on second thought one might wonder how in Italy the general attitude towards the cultural heritage became one of complete, ill-concealed neglect. An indifference capable of transcending also the national borders: not only do we let the archaeological treasures of Pompeii crumble into oblivion day after day and manage to fill in with rubbish the streets of Rome, we even succeed in demolishing the cultural endowments of the other countries. Not something to be proud of, if one bears in mind that the conservation and furtherance of the cultural heritage is addressed in one of the first and most important articles of the Italian Constitution, the so-called *principi fondamentali* ('fundamental principles'). Article No.9 states that "the Republic promotes the development of culture and of scientific and technical research. It safeguards natural landscape and the historical and artistic heritage of the Nation". In one of his many books

Salvatore Settis, the preeminent Italian archaeologist and art historian, wrote that "in the last centuries, right in our country there has been the elaboration of a culture of conservation which is very alert and sophisticated. It has given value to monuments big and small as single parts of a system linked to our territory, a network rich in meaningful repositories of identity in which the value of every single monument or artwork is not determined by its isolation but rather by its assimilation into a vital context. It is this culture that above all has guaranteed the conservation of monuments in Italy more than elsewhere. Foremost it has allowed to perceive and sanction the significance of even the least important monuments. It has given value to such significance by relating them to their original context, to the dense weave of connections with other lesser or superior monuments that throw meaning and light at each other"[6]. Yet, the main subject of his pamphlet is exactly the opposite: the disregard which Italian politicians of left and right alike show for our cultural patrimony. His book makes it dishearteningly clear that gone are the days when the rest of Europe admired Italy not only for its invaluable artistic possessions, but also for the care it put in studying, cataloguing, preserving its trove of paintings, frescoes, sculptures, archaeological finds, churches and palaces of all ages and styles, medieval towns, and all artifacts that bear testimony to Italy's pivotal contribution to the formation and flourishing of the now fading western civilization. The attitude of the average Italian has become one of neglect of or even scorn for all things in the realm of the humanities that can not be conveniently turned into money-making magnets for tourists. Italians revere the Colosseum, the

Uffizi, Piazza San Marco, the tower of Pisa, Caravaggio, Canaletto, Botticelli, everything that comes immediately to mind when one must turn up with a good idea for a postcard from the boot-shaped country. But at the same time we seem to have become oblivious that "the substance of our identity, the network that envelops us and gives us our character is the fact that our cultural patrimony is made up of the cities where we live, the churches we go in, the homes and the palaces that we inhabit or visit, our coasts and our mountains. Our cultural patrimony is not a foreign body tossed in from outside, but something that we have created in the course of time and which we have lived with for generations, century after century. It is not petty cash inside a piggy bank that can be spent if necessary, but our memory, our soul"[7]. People show consideration for the monuments and the artworks that have been celebrated in literature and cinema, the same ones that have been visually appropriated by the rest of the world. But the suspect is that we only preserve what we would be too ashamed to let fall to pieces, frightened as we are that one day some highbrow spokesperson of the foreign intelligentsia might scold us for not being able to look after a treasure that, after all, belongs to the whole human species. Nevertheless, we do not hesitate to turn a blind eye when what is in peril is not located along the main routes of mass tourism or does not yield one of the fine products made in Italy that we do so much to protect on the world market.

Venice is the perfect case study to understand what happens in the entire country. Even if one rules out the big fire that destroyed the Fenice opera house as a criminal deed committed by a couple of morons (in 1996 two electricians who were working in the theatre and were behind schedule had the brilliant idea of setting the building on fire to avoid paying a fine), the city offers many instances of the Italian disregard for the cultural heritage that has become one of the most prominent national traits. The shrug, the typical Italian gesture made to display a total indifference to something, is the perfect physical translation of many people's mindset as regards all the things that stand for our achievements in art, literature, cinema, architecture, and any other occupation of the human intellect. So, although Venetians may pretend to care or even deceive themselves into believing that they really care for their hometown, they do so only when what is at stake is a topnotch monument like Rialto bridge, Piazza San Marco, or Santa Maria della Salute. It is as if their eyes had lost the faculty to register the anonymous details that suffer in silence the consuming touch of time, weather, and man. They do not seem to manage to understand what is stressed by Settis' words: that the works of architects and artists that provide a context for Scala del Bovolo or the church of Santa Maria dei Miracoli are like the accompanying instruments without which the music of the soloists would be just a shrill from a glorious past echoing inside an empty room. Venice is a seamless fabric of architectural and artistic feats. As such, the more it is abused, the more its true colours are destined to fade. If it is not carefully looked after and regularly mended it is bound to come apart and eventually disappear. It takes an amount of money beyond any calculation to keep it together and preserve it for the future generations. Pretending not to be aware of that would be an embarrassing display of naivety. Anybody with a slight knowledge of Italian affairs has peered into the bottomless black hole that looms every time money must be found to save a fresco or simply to carry out some works of basic, ordinary maintenance. But it would be inexcusable to forget that the whole city is a museum en plein air (as is the entire country) and that it should be governed and lived as such. Every now and then someone comes up with the idea that a yearly quota ought to be fixed in order to limit the number of tourists or that they should pay a ticket to have access to Venice, a landing tax that the municipality might start exacting from them as soon as the Covid-19 pandemic is over. Such proposals show that there is some sort of vague awareness of the fragility of the town and of the necessity to ease the pressure put on it by millions of people that use it as a backdrop for the ultimate vacation on the edge of the world and of history: a holiday in the Machu Pichu of Europe to watch it dissolve in real time at the cost of a cheap flight and a few nights in an unregistered b&b. At the same time, it seems that apart from the usual complaints about how stressing it is to walk among the human traffic of Strada Nuova or the impossibility to get on the waterbuses packed up with *foresti* ('foreigners') no serious attempt is ever made by the citizens and the local institutions to safeguard Venice. It surely seems to be of no concern to that vast portion of the population that regards the streets of their own city as open-air toilets for their dogs and never say no to whoever rents their properties to turn them into shops of cheap souvenirs made in countries where working conditions are the same as those experienced by their great-grandfathers. There are a few fierce resistants (Laboratorio Occupato Morion, SaLE Docks, Marco Polo bookshops, No Grandi Navi, Associazione Poveglia, Masegni & Nizioleti), but unfortunately they often do not manage to attain much or end up staging ephemeral displays of civic folklore.

One of the reasons of Venetians' inability to prevent the decadence of their own city might be the simple fact that they were born there. When someone is used since childhood to walk, play, study, work, spend their entire life surrounded by all sorts of natural and man-made expressions of beauty, they may end up taking it all for granted and become insensitive to what is around them. Perhaps beauty is like an intoxicant: if people take it regularly they become accustomed to it and after a while it has no effect on them. The more one is exposed to it, the less he or she will notice it because "our judgement's power to see things is lulled to sleep once we grow accustomed to anything"[8]. Everything is drained of its non-economic value and becomes an empty silhouette in one's daily scenography. Like the buildings in the western movies that have a façade but no depth, Italian historic cities like Venice are such a common landscape for their denizens that they become as insignificant as a word that, when repeated many times, loses its meaning. And such attitude is not as new as one might think. Even John Ruskin, back in the 19th Century when he visited Venice to write his masterpiece, noticed that "you may walk from sunrise to sunset, to and fro, before the gateway of St. Mark's, and you will not see an eye lifted to it, nor a countenance brightened by it. Priest and laymen, soldier and civilian, rich and poor, pass by it alike regardlessly"⁹. It should not surprise that the virus of imperceptiveness infected also the majority of the local politicians and handlers of all public things. After all they are very seldom gifted with superior moral and intellectual qualities. Sometimes they come up with ideas that make one wish that the international community could step in, remove all aborigines from public offices, and appoint a committee of foreign, independent experts to work for the city's welfare. Any policy they might propose to save Venice would be more sensible than the suggestion made in 2015 by the newly elected mayor Luigi Brugnaro (who, like any other mayor of the city, is invested with the honorary title of Vice-President of the Biennale Foundation). He proposed to sell some modern art paintings housed in the museum of Ca' Pesaro to get some pocket money for the municipality. Among the others, he suggested to put on the market the "Rabbino di Vitebsk" by Marc Chagall and the "Giuditta II – Salomè" by Gustav Klimt, the latter considered to be the most precious and definitely the least alienable masterpiece by a non-Italian painter of the entire collection. Declaring in the local dialect that "prima de morir vardando un quadro, vendo el quadro" ('I'd rather sell a painting than starve looking at it'), the mayor estimated that around 400 million euros could be made by getting rid of some expendable artworks. Eventually he did not manage to carry out his business plan. Nonetheless, his ~~indecent~~ modest proposal stretched for a little longer the notoriety he had earned when he engaged in a Twitter squabble with Elton John over the rights of the LGBT community and the same old topic: Venice's inextinguishable need of funds. On that occasion the mayor – who later on would wear a Batman costume and the uniform of Venice's garbage collectors to show the various ways in which he intended to clean up the city - ended up challenging the English pop star to hand out some money to save the city, putting on one of the most despicable shows of brazen scrounging. "Fora i schei!" ('get your money out!'), he ordered Elton John, oblivious of the fact that in 2008 the singer had performed a benefit concert in Piazza San Marco to raise funds for the preservation of the city's main square.

Perhaps the Gods above were trying to drown Brugnaro in order to prevent his election and subsequent international campaign of ridicule when, in September 2014, they sent a pouring rain over the red shingles of Venice. Unfortunately not only did the Gods not succeed in stopping his electoral campaign, but their attempt had also the side effect of damaging some 5,000 art catalogues and magazines stored in the Accademia di Belle Arti in front of the Giudecca island. In truth part of the responsibility for that mishap should be blamed on us mortals, since we did not perform a regular check on the conditions of the roof. In fact, the wind and the rain dislodged part of the sealing on the roof and the water found a way to leak into the first floor and then down the ground floor. The volumes (including one hundred antique books) were drenched with water, some beyond any hope of recovery. The local newspapers reported that the total damage amounted to around 250,000 euros. The fact that they all stressed the cost of the books without mentioning one single title or author makes it clear what is the value that really matters when one speaks of culture. Again, Settis' words sound like a belated admonition: "Nowadays Italy's cultural heritage is degraded to its mere economic value, a commodity that can be disposed of at will. Yet, there is nothing that can measure the well-being of a community as much as the connection that it manages to establish with its monuments and its landscape"[10]. And to prove that the problem is not just a Venetian issue it suffices to say that what happened at the Accaemia di Belle Arti happened at the Pinacoteca di Brera in Milan as well. In April 2019 water leaked from the roof of the gallery and damaged the frame of a painting by Paris Bordon and threatened, luckily unsuccessfully, to fall on some of Rubens' artworks. One might object that in the same days the cathedral of Notre-Dame de Paris was partially destroyed by a fire and that the French disaster was much worse than the water leaks in Italy. However, what in France was a one-off apocalyptical accident appears to be the blueprint for many small Italian tragedies.

Do the boutades of the city's mayor and the disaster of the Accademia di Belle Arti have anything to do with the incident that happened to the Finnish pavilion in 2011? Not directly. Nor does the misbehavior of the citizens and the tourists that dispose of the city as they please. Yet they help picture the backdrop against which the incident took place. It is a social and cultural landscape in which the managing class waits for the problems of the community to get fixed by themselves, all the while muttering the age-old Italian mantra "che Dio ce la mandi buona" ('God help us'). That happens because those in power are almost never held answerable for their shortcomings. On the other hand the commoners are so accustomed to the mishandling of all public patrimony (artistic or not) that they have come to terms with the idea of being speechless spectators of a sort of medieval drama about an inverted world where institutional incompetence, buffoonery, unaccountability, and laxity are the norm. So they keep on dreaming about a utopian future of good governance and when they are confronted with more bad news their reaction is to repeat Billy Pilgrim's adage: "So it goes". That is why a dead tree could fall over the Finnish pavilion even though it could have been prevented. And that is why it passed unnoticed. Thus the philosophical riddle "If a tree falls in a forest and no one is around to hear it, does it make a sound?" remains unanswered, but at least now we know with absolute certainty that the tree does not make any sound even when people are around if they do not care to listen. Fortunately what happened to the Finnish pavilion was remediable and at least it served as a lesson on the opportunity to keep a constant check on the conditions of the flora of the Giardini, especially if potentially deadly. So in due time (five years) a dozen or so rather big trees were cut down because although they looked quite healthy the wood inside had turned into compacted sawdust and might have pulverized at any moment. And year after year a few more are felled. In 2022 alone all the big trees of the main promenade were cut down. Now it would be difficult to say for how long specific trees among those that were felled had been a danger to the visitors and the people working during the various editions of the Art and Architecture Biennale. It would also make no sense at all to wonder how many more months or years some of them might have stood there without harming anybody. So, it would be pure speculation to try to estimate whether the decision to fell a particular tree is well-timed or not. What is really frightening is that probably, unbeknown to the majority of visitors, there might still be a tree that is just waiting to come down.

The Biennale's concepts of timeliness and common sense do not have anything to do with those of the outside world. In 2014 summer was more rainy than usual, especially in July. Many people's vacations in Venice were ruined by a light rain that came down softly, covering the city with a liquid blanket of mild melancholy. The most urgent concern of the majority of managers and exhibition attendants of the various pavilions in the Giardini was to try to keep the floors clean and inevitably to scrub them at the end of the day, after they had been covered with mud by the visitors' shoes, sneakers, boots, sandals, and the always fashionable bare feet. That summer, those who had to go to work before the opening time on rainy days had the chance to witness one of the oddest scenes ever. Surely all fans of Monty Python did appreciate the appalling nonsense of the event, but anybody else in their right minds could not but be struck by what in fact was one of the most untimely waste of money and natural resources. In the Giardini, under a delicate, incessant rain the automatic irrigation system was switched on. For the joy of millions of mosquitoes that would reproduce in the warm ponds of stale water, small faucets popping out from the patches of grass squirted water drops in circles of perfect uselessness. As if the sky alone had not been sufficient to wet the earth, man was trying his best to make sure that the green areas would turn into rice paddies. Perhaps whoever was in charge of the irrigation system thought that a small scale deluge was what was needed to prompt all the urban planners participating in the Architecture Biennale of 2014 to find new solutions to cope with the rising sea level. But all he or she managed to achieve was an accomplished performance in absurdity. Especially so if one bears in mind that the projects exhibited at the Biennale often aim at boosting a collective sensibility towards topics related to economic decrease or rational consumption of natural resources. That waste of water was more appalling than comic considering that the following year the Biennale's sister event was the World Exposition (Expo 2015) held in Milan and presided by Paolo Baratta's sister-in-law. Titled "Feeding the Planet, Energy for Life", its manifesto (the "Milan Charter") made explicit references to "water loss", "sound management of water resources", and "avoiding water wastage in all daily, domestic and productive activities". The document was presented to the UNO as a pledge of a collective commitment to find a solution to problems such as undernourishment and access to unpolluted water, the same element that the Biennale could afford to use in abundance even when not necessary. When I asked one of the gardeners why the sprinkler system was not switched off on rainy days he gave me an obvious reply which confirmed the usual paradigm: "It is automatic and supposed to work every day. It is not in my power to turn it off". Once a decision is taken, rationality is ruled out for good.

Waste is a rather subjective matter. Everyone has their own standards of acceptability and is particularly careful as regards specific materials and resources. Being fond of books, both as repositories of content and as editorial objects, I was struck by a peculiar policy that I got to know when I worked in the bookshop of the Biennale in 2001. Run by Electa, one of Italy's most distinguished publishing houses specialized in art and architecture, the bookstore was already metamorphosing into a gift shop, which is that room that can be found in any public gallery or museum and in which gadgets made of cheap cardboard and oil derivatives erode the space that used to be reserved for books. However, back then the editorial products were still the main attraction. Every volume was picked up, browsed, torn, ripped, blotted with sweat and saliva, put back on the wrong shelf by uncountable pairs of hands. If it did not survive this ordeal and its conditions made it unfit for commerce, any book was destined to be kept as a display copy until the end of the Biennale. Then, I thought, it would be sold for half price, donated to an art school or, I hoped, bestowed upon one of the miserable shop clerks that had to suffer heat in summer, cold in autumn, and occasionally the sewage stink coming from the toilet of the pavilion designed by James Stirling (with the aid of Thomas Muirhead). The structure served as a bookshop for many years but now it is used as a temporary library which is only open during the Biennale. The long building resembles an old steamboat gliding peacefully along a river, which is a moving image if one bears in mind that it is the last project that the Scottish architect completed before passing away in 1992. It is said that he used to supervise the construction site half-drunk, which might explain why he conceived a bookstore without an adequate storeroom to stockpile the several thousand volumes that are sold during every Biennale. It was while working in it in 2001 that I had to face the sad - and to me incomprehensible - truth that all the damaged, unsaleable publications were to be sent to a pulping mill. Perhaps the purpose of that procedure was to prevent the books from being dumped into the market of second hand books. A reasonable explanation for an otherwise unreasonable policy. The following year I worked again in the bookshop, this time in the Arsenale. One day it was discovered that some books were soaked with humidity and would have to be disposed of. Much to anyone's surprise this time the shop assistants had the permission to take home one or two items. I chose a thick, expensive volume whose title, author, and publisher I can not remember. But the blurred memory of its greyish cover is still the objective correlative of a mixed feeling of unfulfilled expectation and of the awareness of being always the weak player in the old game between the employer and the employee. It is a master vs. slave game in which power is displayed in its most extreme form and becomes so unmindful of human relations that it goes as far as withstanding logical thought and acting at variance with its own decisions. What happened was a gratuitous manifestation of the power that Pier Paolo Pasolini defined as anarchic because of its unlimited arbitrariness and its readiness even to contradict itself. A proof that those in power can drag their subordinates into situations of total idiocy and expect them not to question or lament the absurdity of what is going on. Here is what happened. When I finished working I went home with my new book, its pages already wavy because of the humidity.

Along the borders of some of them I could spot yellow stains. Their contours were jagged lines that looked like minuscule fjords where the water had halted its progress into the paper's fibres. Not a big issue. After all I had not paid anything for the book. So I placed it beside a radiator to dry it up, but not too close to it lest the heat might parch the binding and make it crack. Then I reinforced the spine with some vinyl glue so the pages would turn smoothly without coming apart. I did a rather good job and finally the book did look much better than many others sold in second hand stores. I could not imagine that the next day my successful attempt to rescue it from its doom would be frustrated by a few words of the shop supervisor. When I started my shift he informed me that new instructions had been dispatched from the main office in Milan: all damaged books should be sent to the pulping mill, including mine. I relinquished it trying to show no sign of resentment or complain, but being young, educated, and poor I thought (and still do so) that it was a shame to throw away non-marketable books instead of donating them. Moreover, I felt outraged at the lightheartedness with which the company running the bookshop was yo-yoing me. It was one more instance of how easily employers can go back on their word and play with their workers as if they were lobotomized dupes. I had seen the same attitude before and I knew I would see it again in the future. So, I attuned myself to the level of trustworthiness of my employer and retaliated as any young, educated, and poor slave would have done. I felt myself released from my bond of loyalty and retorted with an act that up until then I had never taken into serious consideration: pilferage. I cherry-picked some brand new books straight from the shelves (I can remember a history of architecture with a red dust jacket and something like a study of sacred architecture in the Pacific islands), stashed them in my bag, and went on working without the slightest sense of guilt or shame.

The authority that is not able to fulfil its own propositions and is completely unconcerned about that is just one of the various manifestations of the absolute power that a man or a woman can have over other men and women. It is definitely reproachable, but it is certainly less oppressive than the dictatorial attitude that some employers show when dealing with their employees. In a context like the Biennale, in which good breeding, tolerance, sensitiveness are supposed to be the norm, despotism is rightly perceived by many as pure abuse. One may be surprised at reading that shouting, threats, intimidation, scorn, mobbing, and derision find their way into the world's most famous art exhibition. But the sad truth is that even at the Biennale there are people invested with authority who do not have a clear idea of where they are and could just as well be working in an abattoir or serving as officers in the army. If on one hand there are supervisors on friendly terms with their subordinates and curators that invite to dinner the exhibition attendants of their pavilions, on the other there are firsthand accounts of fearful submission and verbal harassing on a par with Lieutenant Lockhart's speech to the recruits in "Full Metal Jacket". Some people believe that establishing a regime of terror can be a profitable motivational technique to increase the productivity of their staff. They take pleasure in administering a retributive justice. For them any mistake or act of misconduct must be met with a proportionate punishment instead of the plain and simple reprimand that one would expect in a work environment such as the Biennale. It is the case, for example, of the manager of one of the main national pavilions in the Giardini. A couple of his verdicts will be sufficient to fully appreciate the rigor of the discipline he imparts to his staff. One was meted out during a vernissage. Anybody with a minimum of experience of the opening days of the Biennale knows that it would take ten guards per pavilion to make things run smoothly and keep everything under tight control. But since almost every exhibition or special event is understaffed, all attendants' nervous system is put to the test by demanding journalists and annoying self-proclaimed vip's. Moreover, they have to pick up all the empty glasses abandoned here and there, see that the floor is as clean as possible, refill the stacks of information material, turn down intruders' requests to speak with the artists and curators, prevent killjoys from putting on embarrassing unauthorized performances, protect the artworks and the installations from the probing hands of tipsy tactile explorers searching for a secret message written in braille on their surface. The most unfortunate can not even find enough time for a decent lunch break. Very often during the vernissage I have worked almost twelve hours per day, drinking coffee and water on an empty stomach. So, it takes just a little humaneness on the part of the pavilions' managers to understand that mistakes must be weighed with some extra laxity. Indeed most of them do so. But not the aforementioned pavilion manager. He takes so seriously his job, especially as regards disciplinary measures, that one year he made an exhibition attendant pay for a catalogue stolen during the vernissage when the books were under her responsibility. Yet, as regards money another girl fared much worse than that. One day she went to work half an hour late because she had not managed to get on one of the overcrowded waterbuses. As a result she was not paid for the whole working day. Such punishment would not have been uncommon during the Middle Age, but is surely quite objectionable since the proclamation of "The Universal Declaration of Human Rights", whose article No.23 states that "everyone, without any discrimination, has the right to equal pay for equal work" and that "everyone who works has the right to just and favourable remuneration ensuring for himself and his family an existence worthy of human dignity, and supplemented, if necessary, by other means of social protection". That pavilion manager truly makes his collaborators pay for their mistakes. In addition to that he also has a penchant for the good old public humiliation. Once, right in the middle of an amiable staff dinner, he took the chance to chastise a girl - at this point one is led to suspect that he is a bit of a misogynist - for all her supposed shortcomings. As if possessed by Stalin's ghost he staged a public trial in the restaurant, pointing out all the girl's flaws and especially her allegedly poor performance at work. None of her colleagues spoke in her defence for fear of becoming their chief's next victim, thus increasing his feeling of being a demigod of efficiency dispensing blind justice. Had he watched Brian De Palma's "The Untouchables" the night before, he might have been inspired to walk around the table and bash the girl's head with a baseball bat.

The heart of the matter

It would be difficult to state whether the majority of the people employed at the Biennale are happy or not, since there is a continuous turnover of both (few) bosses and (many) underdogs. Some people hold their post for years, whereas many make a quick appearance for just a few weeks. One thing is certain: as regards the relationship between employers and employees the Biennale is no safe haven. There too the former can deal with the latter as they please. After all it is a machine that must work non-stop for six months. If any lumpenprole of the art world is unhappy and wants to quit it takes just a few hours to find an overqualified substitute.

Some workers of the lower ranks manage or need to keep their jobs for some years, others come and go in one season. So do the key players of the Biennale, that is to say the artists, the curators, and the directors without whom the whole thing would not even exist. Some of them are completely unknown outside the art world, some others are real and proper celebrities. Some go unnoticed during the exhibition and leave no trace behind when it is all over, others are remembered for what they do or simply for what they are. The people who work in the Giardini and in the Arsenale have the opportunity to meet them or at least to see them more frequently than the general public. Obviously many celebrities come to the Biennale as visitors and some of them do it regularly. They too are remembered for their kindness or their rudeness. Some are aloof, others friendly, but for people like me it is always difficult to approach a famous person and find anything to say that will not sound naive. I have never dared tell David

Byrne that I believe that his and Brian Eno's "My Life in the Bush of Ghosts" is one of the musical masterpieces of the late 20th Century, or inform the heavily tattooed Swiss art critic Etienne Dumont how much I admire his boldness. I was not able to find anything smart to say to the Nobel laureate John Maxwell Coetzee when he signed a book for me, neither did I ever tell the late Italian politician Paolo Bonaiuti how surprising it was that he seemed to be genuinely interested in contemporary art. He who had been spokesman for the most boorish Italian Prime Minister after Benito Mussolini, namely Silvio Berlusconi, the man who did so much to debase intellectuals and barbarize Italian culture. But I did not hesitate to introduce myself to Luc Tuymans when I found him eating a sandwich in the pavilion where I worked. He was the official curator of the exhibition, although it would be more correct to define his role as 'spiritual guidance', i.e. he lent his name to boost the appeal of the exhibition and make the artworks more saleable. Out of hunger or perhaps pure indifference to my person, he seemed to be so absorbed in his sandwich that he registered my presence there as much as that of a fly on a wall. In fact, when I approached him to shake hands with the sole purpose to annoy him with my existence, he stared at me with the eyes of a gallerist who is about to close a good deal with a collector but is suddenly interrupted by someone who wants to ask information about an artwork that is glaringly out of their reach. Eyes that give out a mix of muffled irritation, disdain, and pity. This notwithstanding, fate offered me the chance to make some money thanks to him. Or at least I thought so when I found an almost full bottle of Jack Daniel's in the pavilion and someone told me that it had been bought and forgotten there by Tuymans himself. I immediately had the idea of selling it on Ebay, bids starting from 500 euros. Or I might have stored it until his death to put it on the market when his memorabilia would have been more profitable. Unfortunately after he left I never dared contact him and ask him to sign a certificate of authenticity, so I kept the bottle on a shelf in the pavilion for a few years until one fine day I realized that it had disappeared. Probably someone had found it and, being unaware of its real value, had drunk it up to forget the pains and troubles of the Biennale.

Another celebrity - if that is the right word to define a monarch - that I had the chance to meet and shake hands with was Jonkvrouw Mathilde d'Udekem d'Acoz, aka Queen Mathilde of Belgium. Obviously when we were introduced to each other I said the wrong thing, something like "I am pleased to meet you, Madam" (which she might have found rather disrespectful). But all the other ways to address her that I had come up with in my mind – such as "I am honoured to meet you, Your Highness" or "Your Grace, I am your humble servant" - sounded ridiculously passé or servile. However, being an exhibition attendant, I was the last person that she might have wanted to engage in conversation, so our encounter lasted about three seconds and then she went on to meet other people who fitted into that sort of situation much more than I. She shook everybody's hand and then went on to speak with the artist and the curator, who gave her a private tour of the show. Obviously President Baratta was with her, but he touched only a narrow selection of hands from which mine was unsurprisingly excluded. In her light-coloured, unpretentious outfit and pillbox hat the Queen reminded me of Jackie Kennedy, while her modest retinue and security detail were in sharp contrast with many Italian politicians' habit of using an unnecessary number of attendants and bodyguards with the only purpose of adding strength to their public image (the irony being that very often the more they affirm to be loved by the people the more bodyguards they seem to need to be protected from them). But such lack of pomposity did not mean that the Queen's visit had not been carefully planned. In fact, security measures and logistical arrangements had been carefully thought over well in advance, so much so that even I had been requested to participate in a briefing with the exhibition's curator, the Belgian ambassador, the prefect of Venice, the chief of the city's constables, and some other officials and officers. The meeting had not lasted very long, less than one hour. Any relevant issue had been discussed and dealt with quite quickly and easily. Except one: what to do in case we would be confronted by the urgency of a royal pee? The Queen could not possibly be supposed to use the public lavatories in the Giardini, considering that every day they were used by hundreds of visitors and therefore they would have fallen short of meeting the basic standards of décor and privacy which befit a royal toilet. Therefore, it had been decided to tidy up and gild the pavilion's tiny restroom as best as possible. Of course it would also have to be kept locked until our guest would leave in order to prevent anybody from using and messing it. So, the cleaning company that had been contracted to scrub and mop the floor of the exhibition rooms had been asked to make sure that the toilet would be restored to its pristine condition – that is an ideal state in which very probably it had never been seen by anybody. They did a good job and with the aid of a few props bought by the artist's assistant the restroom looked like the toilet of a small but cozy room of a three star hotel. The floor was adorned with a dark green fluffy carpet and on the sink, to the left of the tap, were laid a couple of lily-white hand towels while to its right there was an unopened dispenser of moisturizing amber hand soap. Eventually the toilet did not receive the state visit it had been spruced up for, so it was left to me to enjoy its royal lushness in the following days. A couple of years later I was graced again with the same royal visit, but much to my relief another toilet was prepared for the occasion.

I too was a celebrity in 2009, although just for a couple of minutes and my fans did not even know who I was. It happened when an American photographer asked me if she could take my portrait inside the pavilion. She said that she was working on a series of portraits of exhibition attendants and other personnel of the Biennale and that her intention was to exhibit the prints during the next edition of the show. I eagerly consented to her request, partly to help her and partly because I fancied her. So, I sat on a chair behind the white desk from which I used to sell catalogues and distribute information material while she framed my face with the lens of her expensive 6x7 Mamiya film camera. I tried to look as detached and unembarrassed as possible, but this had the side effect of making the visitors in the room think that I was the artist or another famous person they had not seen or heard of before. Yet that made no difference to them: a photographer with professional equipment was shooting pictures of me, which meant that for some obscure reason I had to be someone important and that was enough to start them taking snapshots of me. Some of them looked puzzled by my face but they did not want to loose the chance of having their own picture of a celebrity. Others had an expression of delightful surprise on their faces, as if they had been hoping all their life to see me in the flesh. In about two minutes a dozen people scrambled to capture my physical features without enquiring about my identity. Certainly it took them just two more minutes to forget about me and eventually they deleted my face from their memory cards and their own minds. I was happy to plunge back into my comforting anonymity.

Everybody picks up their favourite director of the Biennale, the most impolite art celeb, the kindest curator, the most arrogant architect, the most good-looking performer, any person that stands out for a positive or for a negative trait. As far as I am concerned, I would give the golden lion for snobbery to whom was the very king of the Biennale: Paolo Baratta. During his tenure of the presidency from 2008 to 2020 I spent eleven consecutive years in the same pavilion in the Giardini and he did not smile or say hello to me once. I did not expect him to know my name or remember my face. I was happy to be a perfect stranger to him, nonetheless I believe that whoever is on top has the moral obligation to show some empathy to those who find themselves towards the bottom of the social ladder. Even more so if they work in the same environment. The fact that in over a decade the thought of saying hello to the person working in that pavilion (even if it had been a different person every year) never crossed his mind might have been due to a severe case of absent-mindedness. Or perhaps the reason might have been that notwithstanding its cosmopolitanism and apparent finesse the world of contemporary art is led by a ruling class that, far from being as enlightened and progressive as it likes to depict itself, is still fond of a human cosmography in which the elites and the common people must be at the opposite ends of the galaxy. Daniel Birnbaum, the director of the 2009 edition of the Biennale - titled "Making Worlds" - was not of that opinion. He never failed to say hello or smile even when running into the most inconspicuous person. Massimiliano Gioni (2013, "The Encyclopedic Palace") was not as friendly as him, but at least he curated the most accessible Biennale of the recent past. Even the logo and the official posters depicting a head bursting with ideas were much better than the designs seen in the last few years. The lettering of the posters of the 2015 edition, for instance, seemed borrowed from the official merchandising of the "Fast and Furious" movie saga. Directed by Okwui Enwezor (the first-ever black director, because the Biennale wanted its Barak Obama, too) and titled "All The World's Futures", it was one of the most cryptical and low-spirited exhibitions ever held in Venice - perhaps because in that very year Enwezor was diagnosed with the disease that would lead to his premature death in 2019. It was rumoured that the real title should have been "All the World's Wounds" - the deepest one being that suffered by the director himself - and that it was altered by President Baratta in order to make it less gloomy and more marketable. It does not take a genius to understand that the image of a wound and the idea of the future do not tickle people's imagination in the same way. Which means that if the title was really changed the visitors' were suggested a perspective on the exhibition that was completely different from that intended by the director. In addition, although the show covered topical issues through the works of prominent artists, it resulted hard to process by anyone who did not have a mind trained to chew and digest the art practices that address the brain much more than the eyes and the other senses. They are the bastard sons of the most impenetrable cultural monster of the 20th Century: conceptualism. Unfortunately the majority of the good artworks exposed at the Biennale are conceptual in nature, since they struggle not to be understood. They are never self-explanatory. It is as if their authors were taking advantage of what John Berger said, i.e. that "if, on the other hand, you take a very limited view it is possible to sympathize with almost all artists. If you accept what they themselves are trying to do, you can admire their effort. The work is then no longer proof of the validity of the artist's intentions: his intentions have to prove the validity of his work"[11]. So, the poor observer always has to read an A4 sheet of paper, study the critical essays of the catalogue, connect to an ad hoc website in order to come up with a faint idea of their meaning. If in the past centuries artworks were easily understood thanks to a basic knowledge of the Bible, if their narratives could be grasped also by the illiterates who did not have a clue of their underlying metaphors or of the classical mythology which inspired them, nowadays the impression is that they aim at communicating ideas that would be better expressed in words but this is prevented by their authors' refusal or inability to phrase them in the linear, sequential structure of an essay. Someone may object that an art installation is more direct than a book, yet all its power cannot but be lost if its message is not intelligible. This does not mean that the artists should turn into writers or produce purely decorative and figurative works. Rather, it explains why contemporary art is a self-referential world that speaks in code and manages to engage the wide public only when it offers cheap entertainment or big events such as the Biennale, whose success is mainly due to the fact that its visitors regard it as a theme park where there is always a chance to have some fun. What they are after is not simply art, but entARTainment. For most of them a quick selfie with the cast of Sarah Lucas' smoking pussy makes it worth spending an afternoon wandering among inscrutable artworks. On their part, most artists and curators aim only at impressing their peers or perhaps they are simply so used to live on a plan so far removed from that of the common man that they behave like a 50's sci-fi movie's ethereal alien race gifted with a superior mind. They land on Earth to bring light, advanced knowledge, a new perceptiveness, but they can not make themselves be understood by the brutes they encounter on their way. Very often their references to the masters of the past and their tributes to unheard of minor artists do not ring any bells with the public. Likewise, their trans-disciplinary leaps go undetected for six months. So, their installations become esoteric structures that only a few people are equipped to interpret while their multilayered message is flattened by those who have no depth perception. Perhaps that is why in 2019 Ralph Rugoff titled his Biennale "May You Live in Interesting Times": he was speaking directly to its visitors to inform them that he hoped they could make some sense of it and would not get too bored.

The Architecture Biennale has its stars, too. The director of the 2016 edition ("Reporting from the Front") was the Chilean architect Alejandro Aravena. As soon as he was appointed he was hailed as the sex symbol of the architecture of the 3rd Millennium. Perhaps his hot latino look and his grizzled, perfectly rebellious hairdo à la MTV were chosen to clear the air of the sulphur stench left behind two years before by the bald, cold looking Rem Koolhaas. Aravena was slim, he had a beautiful wife, his Biennale was socially aware and addressed ethical issues. Above all, he had eyes that could pin a woman to the wall. Probably none of the girls working at the Biennale in 2016 could mention one single project signed by Aravena, but whenever he walked on the main promenade of the Giardini many of them abandoned their workplace to look at him in awe. Among them there was a hormonal exhibition attendant who got so carried away as to fantasize about a love story with him and make it public through a *fotoromanzo* (a sort of graphic novel with photographs instead of drawings that was popular among Italian housewives from the 50's to the 80's). Every few days she posted on Facebook a picture of Aravena that she had found in the internet and added below it an imaginary short dialogue between herself and her Chilean sweetheart. Obviously the conversation always ended with the same old happy end of the traditional chick lit: no matter what, he was in love with her and nothing could have parted them. Her sketches became so popular that also the high ranks of the Foundation got word about them. So, at the closing party of the Biennale held in Ca' Giustinian they gave her the opportunity to meet Aravena in person and be more close to him than she could ever have imagined. Finally her dream came true, she was introduced to her Romeo who kissed her chastely on her cheek and for one night she felt like the princess of the Biennale. Good for her, who in her few minutes of popularity managed to attract the cheers of her colleagues and offer some amusement to Baratta and his courtiers while her friends and the official photographer of the Foundation took pictures of the romance unfolding in the room. It goes without saying that she later posted the images on Facebook as a proof that the magic had really happened and she, Venetian Cinderella, had finally exchanged a few words with her Prince Charming. All the blue-eyed attendees (a lot, since there were many people in their twenties, either of age or of mental faculties) thought that for one brief moment the social, professional, and hierarchical barriers had crumpled to reveal that the distance between who is on top and who is at the bottom is not unbridgeable. Perhaps they believed that every time a number of persons share the same experience all their differences and prejudices disappear to give place to an interclass milieu of like-minded equals. Other people at the party saw a different scene. They saw the President and his retinue toying with a girl delighted to be their favourite pet for the night. She was all too ready to sell out her self-respect to the very same people for whom she had been nothing for six months, the very same people that would never have bothered to look through her cv had she tried to apply for a job at the Foundation. Shakespeare's fools are wiser than their kings, but that cheap comedy in Ca' Giustinian showed that real life does not always work in accordance with great literature: fools end up embarrassing themselves to let their kings have a merry time and the last laugh.

The Biennale is such a huge event with so many people that one hears all sorts of rumours, gossips, innuendos, legends, stories, slander. Some of them will remain blurred forever, unvalidated by the sworn testimony of an eye witness. We will never know whether it is true or not that Paolo Baratta, when in Ca' Giustinian, refused to share the elevator with a cleaning lady. Or if it is true that one of the top officials of the Foundation can not utter a single word in English and so has all her emails to foreign correspondents translated by her underlings. Who knows if one of the most famous art curators born in the Old Continent, now dead, really started dancing on a table when on 9/11 he was informed that two planes had crashed on the Twin Towers. And can anyone confirm the rumour that in 2011 part of the artists in the collective show of the Italian pavilion bribed some of the sub-curators chosen by Vittorio Sgarbi, the official curator, in order to be selected to exhibit their works? These tales and many more will never be confirmed. But I have listened to a lot of other stories as told by friends or long time colleagues of mine who saw the events or were even involved in them. Therefore I tend to buy into their genuineness. Especially when they are about the same person and they all depict that person in the same way, thus sounding as substantiating each other. It is the case, for instance, of Rem Koolhaas. The Dutch architect and his entire family have a special relationship with Venice and the Biennale. In 2010 he was awarded the Golden Lion for lifetime achievement and in 2014 he curated one of the best exhibitions ever held in the Central pavilion of the Giardini. Its title was "Elements of Architecture" and was part of "Fundamentals", the Architecture Biennale directed by him. The aim of the show was to go back to basics, to the very foundations of architecture. The visitors could walk from one thematic room to another, from "Floor" to "Corridor", from "Toilet" to "Escalator", from "Door" to "Roof", and end up in the amazing, breathtaking "Window", whose items were borrowed mainly from the Brooking National Collection. In 2008 a rare animated movie entitled "Flagrant Délit" made in the 70's by his first wife, Madelon Vriesendorp, was screened in the Central Pavilion. Four years later his second wife, Petra Blaisse, was chosen to represent the Netherlands during the 13th Architecture Biennale. She exhibited a huge curtain sliding across the pavilion, a piece of moving furniture that for many interior designers is the furniture par excellence. In 2016 his son Tomas' movie premiered at the 73rd edition of the cinema festival. It is a documentary titled "REM". It does not take a genius to guess whose life and work it is about (a hint: it is not about Michael Stipe's band). But this is not all. Together with Santiago Calatrava (the designer of the infamous Ponte della Costituzione, the fourth bridge over the Canal Grande that, when it is wet, makes pedestrians feel like they are skating on ice) Rem Koolhaas is one of the few architects that have significantly altered the urbanistic and architectural structure of Venice in the 21st Century. In fact, he is the mastermind behind the restoration of Fontego dei Tedeschi, a palace in front of Rialto bridge built in 1228 that later served as Venice's central post office. In 2016 the *palazzo* ('palace') was reopened as a luxury shopping mall, which reveals a lot about the mentality of those who have the power to decide the new course that the city of Venice must take - at this point it is worth reminding that one year later mayor Luigi Brugnaro stated that it was his intention to turn Venice into a European version of Dubai, as if the city needed to borrow its identity from another one. Fontego dei Tedeschi is still one of the biggest buildings in town and is located right at its centre, but unfortunately its new function is the most antihistorical endeavour ever taken in a city unable to make sense of itself. The very idea of having a monument to the idol of luxury when the western world's population is becoming more poor than it can remember is absurd. Even more so in Venice, where the majority of the over 20 million yearly tourists choking the city streets are happy to buy a cheap mask for the price of one espresso or some fake Murano glass made in China. Certainly the members of the governing board of DFS Group, the Hong Kong based company that owns the Fontego (renamed T Fondaco), expect that the rich Russian morons and the even richer Arabs that shop at the Prada and Louis Vuitton stores behind Museo Correr also spend some money in their mausoleum of luxury goods. For sure that happens every day, but what they probably prefer not to think about is that most of the people inside the building refurbished by Rem Koolhaas are passersby that step in just to look around or to find a toilet. Probably they would be surprised to know that the city's residents and visitors appreciate the smartly dressed young men that open the doors to let them in and the headache inducing perfume that is sprayed in the lobby far less than the opportunity to use free, luxurious public lavatories. What was conceived as a new big shopping venue different from, even opposed to the tiny stores of crap souvenirs of Strada Nuova has ended up being a public toilet for the very same people it was not supposed to serve. At least it offers a public service, plus an amazing vista of the town from its terrace. Yet one may wonder if an architecture celebrity like Rem Koolhaas really needed to lend his name to the transformation of a historical building into a glittering replica of the duty free area of Marco Polo airport. Perhaps he was oblivious of the fact that in a city like Venice buildings are like the paintings in a gallery, that "what happens when a new work of art is created is something that happens simultaneously to all the works of art which preceded it. The existing monuments form an ideal order among themselves, which is modified by the introduction of the new (the really new) work of art among them. The existing order is complete before the new work arrives; for order to persist after the supervention of novelty, the whole existing order must be, if ever so slightly, altered; and so the relations, proportions, values of each work of art toward the whole are readjusted; and this is conformity between the old and the new… the past should be altered by the present as much as the present is directed by the past"[12]. Obviously he did not work for money and it is hard to believe that he was hungry for fame, since he is the most famous architect in the world. The only good reason for getting involved in the project must have been his own ego. The chance to lay his hands on Venice meant that he could cement his professional legacy into one of the most famous cities of the planet. A unique city, very much unlike London, New York, Beijing, Moscow, Dubai, or any other that can come to mind inasmuch as it is stuck in time and no one has the boldness or the authorization to go much further than to restore a flat or renovate a shop. Apart from what was done by Carlo Scarpa (much for the Biennale itself, for instance the Venezuelan pavilion and the old ticket booth) almost nothing has been built or heavily modified in Venice in the last century. Making anything new or altering what was made when architecture was still an occupation more fit to artists than to engineers is like working on the pyramids of Giza or the Taj Mahal. It means attempting to adulterate something that, perfect or not, is an accomplishment of a long gone culture and as such must be preserved until an alien superior civilization has proved itself able to reach the same heights of architectonic expression. Which makes sense especially in Italy, where there is an overlong list of unfinished public architecture and what is brought to completion is very seldom comparable with what was made in the past or is currently being made in other countries. Moreover, the very identity of Venice rests in every single brick of the walls that reject with salt and humidity all human attempts to rejuvenate them with a layer of cosmetic plaster and paint. On every *masegno* ('stone slab') trod by millions of shoes one can read a paragraph of its history. Any column capital is a photograph carved in stone of the tastes of an epoch and many architraves remind of the ties that the republic of La Serenissima had with remote lands that up until not long ago seemed to belong more to the field of fantastic literature than to that of geography. Venice is like a giant living creature, alas dormant, that bears its DNA code written on its skin: to modify its exterior, what is most visible of it, means to alter its nature and identity. If it could speak, it would borrow a line from one of the characters in Wim Wenders' "Kings of the Road". When asked who he is, he replies "I am my story". That is why building something as imposing as a new bridge across the Canal Grande or carrying out massive restoration works such as those which affected the Fontego is an act of extreme courage. Any sensible architect appointed to accomplish the task must inevitably be gripped by the fear of defacing the city and erecting a monument to their own disgrace. But for those with an unshakable self-esteem the temptation is irresistible. Leaving one's mark in the most unique city in the world is worth more than any commission that may come from the Louvre or the Hermitage. It goes far beyond the current idea of celebrity: it means engraving one's name in history. With the Fontego Rem Koolhaas managed to achieve this goal. Time will tell whether he added a new good paragraph to the story of Venice or just an inopportune digression.

So, Rem Koolhaas and his family seem to be everywhere in Venice, especially in and around the Architecture Biennale. He pops up in blogs, books, magazines, videos, seminars, conversations, anywhere. The shapes of the

Guggenheim Museum of Bilbao, London's Gherkin, the Louvre's pyramid, Sydney's Opera House entered pop culture many years ago and anybody could tell what and where they are. Yet nowadays Koolhaas is much more famous than Frank Gehry, Norman Foster, Ieoh Ming Pei, and Jørn Utzon put together despite the fact that very few people, including those working at the Biennale, could mention one single project bearing his studio's stamp that could be deemed as iconic as those of his colleagues. Like Ai Weiwei, he is ubiquitous and it seems like no event can happen in his disciplinary field if there is not at least some allusion to him. So, his name is known even by people without any knowledge of architecture (like myself, who had to look up in Wikipedia to find out who designed the Louvre's pyramid and Sydney's Opera House). It has become as familiar as a brand of mass-produced sneakers or the name of the most popular fizzy drink that can be found in any eating joint the world over. So much so that I instinctively nicknamed him Rem Coca-Koolhaas.

It was during some conversations with other persons working at the Biennale that I happened to listen to a number of hair-rising stories about the Dutch architect that sounded excerpted from a biography of Vlad the Impaler. One of them tells that during the preparation of "Elements of Architecture" he used to be so hard on the interns and young professionals working for his studio that they did not dare ask him for an extra ream of paper for the printer and preferred to beg help and use the facilities of the Biennale's library. They were literally frightened by the idea of not been able to comply with the standards of efficiency set by their boss. And they were right to be so, if one is to believe the account of the young man working at the entrance of the Arsenale who said that he was grabbed by his neck by the architect when he dared prevent him from getting in without a valid badge. Or if one believes the account of the personnel of the ticket booths who affirmed that he kicked their kiosks in a fit of rage when he was informed that nobody had prearranged free tickets for his family. In order to avoid such incidents, in 2014 a black and white print of his portrait was taped to the wall of the green cubicle used by the security guards to check the identity and the badges of the hundreds of people working in the Giardini before the official opening of the Architecture Biennale. Under the photograph, to prevent anybody from getting in his way and unleash the beast, someone (presumably from Ca' Giustinian) had written with a marker pen "Never stop this man!".

At the Biennale some people are mistreated, others are underpaid or simply frustrated by a dull job. It seems just fair that at the end of the exhibition the Foundation throws a cocktail party in Ca' Giustinian to redress wrongs big and small. It is also a good way to further a positive narrative and reassure the lower ranks that they too are part of the extended family of contemporary art and architecture. Obviously from a leftist political stance it is sad to witness how the working class can still be manipulated to help the powers that be write a story that can be easily sold to the world outside. It is also sad to attend a party where the bouncers, who in the early 20th Century would have been called fascist thugs, look down on the participants as freaks of nature that should be sterilized. One year one of them had a good go at me and another guy who was drawing a toy rifle on a desk with a pencil. He ordered us both (I wondered why me as well) to clean the desk on the spot, so the unfortunate illustrator made the drawing disappear to the point that the following day it would have taken the cleaning ladies five seconds to finish the job. However, the bouncer did not seem satisfied and kept on harassing us, finally threatening to break our arms if we would not restore it to its pristine conditions. Luckily it was around midnight, when the party ends and all the attendants are swept out of Ca' Giustinian, so we were saved by a flood of people reaching for the exit.

Brutality notwithstanding it is hard to say no to free alcohol and I must admit that I am a regular guest at the closing party (though mainly to see my friends and colleagues). I too queue at the open bar which is set up in the middle of the main room while a dj plays lousy music. From behind it booze of poor quality is handed out by bartenders who cannot rest for one single minute. And the more people drink, eat, flirt, dance, and laugh the happier is the echelon of the Foundation, for "the fact that most of those taking part in these affairs are temporarily dehumanized by herd-poison is of no account in comparison with the fact that their dehumanization can be used to consolidate the religious and political powers that be"[13]. A crowd is always necessary to the Biennale. To see it, to work in it, to celebrate it, to talk and write about it. Provided that the narrative is suggested by the Biennale itself.

Chapter 2: We're only in it for the money

There are two things in which we Italians love to pride ourselves. One is food. Rich, tasty, varied, the cuisine of the Mediterranean peninsula is famous worldwide and nobody holding an Italian passport could do without it. No matter how small the planet has become, most Italians have never tasted any foreign food other than the usual Chinese and Indian recipes tailored to suit western palates. So confident are most Italians that what they eat at home is the best food that they do not feel the curiosity to try something different. The second thing we like to boast about is that every year tens of millions of foreign tourists flock to our country in order to admire the very same artistic and cultural riches that we seldom set eyes on. Indeed, although it has ups and downs, tourism is always thriving thanks to the uncountable Italian natural and manmade treasures. Certainly the Covid-19 pandemic imposed a set of restrictions and a palpable fear of travelling, yet tourism can only be slowed down but never fully stopped. And Venice is the touristic city par excellence, for better or worse. It could not possibly sustain itself without the over 20 million *foresti* that every year pay a visit to its fewer than 55,000 resident citizens. The locals are not enough to keep the city alive and could never manage to sustain it on their own. The Biennale itself is a tribute to foreign power and creativity. The main venue of the Giardini, for instance, is located inside a public garden that was created in 1807 by Napoleon Bonaparte, who decreed the reclamation of a marshland area in order to endowed the city with a green lung. And should one day the national pavilions withdraw their participation in the exhibition, the Biennale would be left with the Italian pavilion and the main show curated by its director. Surely not enough to attract hundreds of thousands of visitors, as was proved in 2020, when only the Central pavilion and part of the Arsenale were open because of the Covid-19 pandemic. They attracted as many visitors as any common exhibition held in a small private gallery, making it clear that without the national pavilions and the collateral events the Biennale would look like Las Vegas without casinos: a desert. It is the foreigners who throw all the parties during the opening days, summon gallerists and press professionals from all over the world, organize panel discussions and workshops with their artists and curators, provide the bookshop with something to sell other than the general catalogue and the designer gadgets. The Foundation offers the packaging and the brand identity, the national pavilions offer most of the product to sell to the public. It is a symbiosis that is made more conspicuous during winter, when all countries sail out of Venice and the Foundation hibernates without funding a workshop or a panel discussion for about half of the year.

 Venice has become an expanding archipelago of hotels, hostels, b&b's, restaurants, wine bars, pubs, pizzerias, kebab houses, money exchangers, souvenir shops, ice cream and fruit salad stalls. Visitors are offered all sorts of services and entertainments: thematic walking tours, Italian lessons, classical music concerts inside churches, kayak rides in the canals, wedding ceremonies, photography workshops at dawn, flights by helicopter along its perimeter, visits to its museums, galleries, and monuments. It is by serving the tourists in one way or another that most of the people in Venice earn their living. Not everybody owns a hotel or has the right connections or blood ties to claim membership to the two de facto guilds that make good money by fetching the tourists to and from the airport on a watertaxi or by carrying them around town on a gondola. The majority of the people have to work as concierge, waiters, cleaning ladies, bellboys, cooks, dishwashers, bartenders, cashiers in the souvenir shops. All such jobs are respectable and guarantee a fixed income (though very often quite low) and a sense of security. However, they do not have much appeal on those who have dedicated their youth to the study of the humanities. Many young adults holding a degree in philosophy, history of art, archaeology, foreign languages, literature, architecture live in a limbo of soft unemployment. Their life is made up of months or years of employment interspersed by long periods of idleness. No matter how many sermons the politicians, the intellectuals, the enlightened entrepreneurs deliver to praise the Italian cultural patrimony: those who are qualified to preserve and promote it will always be looked upon as slackers, losers, useless dreamers, blue-eyed parasites that did not have the guts to study really useful subjects such as economics or informatics in order to gain a deep knowledge of them and then buy a one way ticket to find a decent job in another country. The best thing they can hope for is a public examination for a post as press officer or white collar in one of the private or public museums of the city, or maybe for a position behind a desk in an institution with a vague connection to culture like Ca' Foscari or IUAV (the city's university and architecture school, respectively). But they know that the odds are 99% that the person who will be given the job has been chosen long before the notice is posted on the institution's website. The last time I tried to apply for a job at the local university I catastrophically failed the written test. The astonishing low mark I was given raised my suspicion so I contacted the university and had a scan of my test sent to me. I found out that not one single mistake had been pointed out in it: it had not even been read by the commission, which clearly had given it a random mark. So I sent another email to the university's dean and the supervisory board to inform them of the malfeasance that I unearthed. To this day I am still waiting for a reply.

Some people, including myself, make the desperate attempt to submit their unsolicited cv "to the kind attention" of the Foundation's human resources department, but it seems like that what people at Ca' Giustinian most appreciate of a resume is the white reverse page to doodle on while chatting on the phone. The suspicion is that one's skills and previous jobs are duly scrutinized only if he or she is a friend of a friend of someone already working for the Foundation, whose recruiting procedure appears to comply with the old Italian blueprint: personal ties and camaraderie weigh in and are often the only prerequisites that can make a difference to succeed in one's job hunt.

For many would-be intellectuals and artists living in or near Venice the only chance to taste a flavourless morsel of the cake is to find a job as an exhibition attendant or shop assistant in a giftshop inside a museum. Not exactly what they dreamed of when they enrolled at the Accademia di Belle Arti or at the university, but still better than serving microwaved pasta to tourists trying to locate the Fontana di Trevi on a city map. So, they wait for the Biennale as a recurrent opportunity to make ends meet. Good for them that, in spite of its name, it happens every year: its two major editions, Art and Architecture, alternate each other. Every earth's journey around the sun is split into two parts of almost equal length: one (from spring to late November) brings some respite to their quest for a job, the other (the remaining months) plunges them again into a state of suspended animation. Some go back to studying, others take the chance to spend the little money they have saved to travel (Asia being one of their favourite destinations), others still take satisfaction in being on the dole until the next Biennale. Those who manage to work every year develop a premodern sense of time. They lose their ability to conceive of time as a continuum of events progressing like an infinite line with no beginning nor end. For them it could be more aptly represented by a circle. The coming and going of the Biennale, the regular succession of working and non-working seasons make their existence go on in cycles of activity and inactivity, labour and idleness, economic security and dire straits. Their lives are trapped in the spokes of a wheel that keeps on spinning and taking them back to the same position every six months or so.

Not only are career opportunities non-existent, the most intelligent boys, girls, men, and women who work at the Biennale for more than a few years - like myself - feel worn off in body and mind like an old audio tape that keeps on being rewound to play the same song over and over again. Meanwhile their colleagues equipped with a less performing brain complain about their job but are secretly in love with an occupation that requires of them little time and effort and is often followed by an unemployment benefit when the Biennale is over.

I worked at the bookshop, both in the Giardini and in the Arsenale. I have a memory of myself and my colleagues as a team of unpretentious people. Nowadays it looks like that most of the personnel of the two bookshops, being surrounded by books printed by publishers big and small, feel like being the keepers of the Royal Library of Alexandria. In their little corner of borgesian heaven they stock the catalogues of almost all the national pavilions plus any other publication that has any chance to be sold, including remainders among which it is possible to find some good bargains. Perhaps it is because of their proximity to so much knowledge that most sales assistants look down on other people like they were Spanish missionaries meeting a tribe of South American heathens in the 16th Century. Notwithstanding their snobbish attitude it is most unfortunate that, as of the writing of this book, even if they are irreproachable professionals they must be ditched after one single Biennale because due to the Italian labour laws the same employer can not hire them for the same seasonal job more than once. Otherwise their employer - which as far back as I can remember has always been Electa, a branch of Mondadori, probably the biggest publishing house in Italy - would be compelled to give them a regular position, but there is simply no need for them when the Biennale is over.

The tour guides hired by the Foundation do not fare much better. They do not earn really a lot for having to adjust their daily chores to a working schedule that is permanently liable to retouches due to a number of variables, from a vip's unpredicted visit to a number of last minute bookings. Every year they do the same thing: during the first week they gather as much information as possible about a few exhibitions, they share it with their colleagues, and finally they bestow it upon school children and students of all grades, groups of art lovers, politicians, a few celebrities, anybody who thinks that a five minutes explanation by a living caption can unveil the mystery of a piece of contemporary art. Usually a tour lasts about one hour and varies depending on the age and level of education of the participants. While the Central pavilion in the Giardini and the Corderie in the Arsenale are a must, the rest of the visit is spent wherever it is most suitable for any specific group. So, everybody sees their national pavilion, kids are taken to see the funniest shows, the elderly kept at a distance from what might give them a headache. What really matters for the guides, especially the least experienced, is that nobody asks any question whose answer is not already formulated in the information material he or she has been reading. The most dreaded thing is a prying visitor who challenges them, albeit involuntarily, to connect the artwork they are looking at with a concept or event unmentioned in the catalogue. Even if the guide has a personal understanding that might help to contextualize or better explain the meaning of the artwork, the peremptory command is to stick to what is written in the catalogue. Not a word in excess must be uttered, lest the orthodoxy of the official publication be contaminated with the knowledge of a heretic guide. They do not imagine that many essays in the books they read are not addressed to those who want to understand but to those who already know, those who are aware that without their obscurity such texts would lose a great deal of their value. After so many years at the Biennale and having looked through many official publications I am sure that a good portion of the curators and scholars who write introductions and all accompanying texts speak mainly to their peers and seek their complicity, confiding that "those who have been inducted into the subtle art of unwrapping portents and unknotting them would be able to find anything they wish in any piece of writing whatsoever: but their game is particularly favoured by the obscure, ambiguous, fantastical jargon of these prophecies, the authors of which never supply any clear meaning themselves so that posterity can give them any meaning it chooses"[1]. One can picture the guides during the opening days, when the information to absorb is much and time is short, spending their nights trying to learn by heart convoluted statements and insubstantial concepts expressed in an over-specialized jargon in order to make them sound more authoritative. One can almost see them, backs bent on the holy scriptures of the catalogues and press releases, swinging their heads like the Afghan kids forced by the Talibans to memorize surahs whose meaning they can only grasp in a distorted, superficial interpretation. Finally, once they have done their homework, they master the essentials of all the exhibitions that are worth seeing and, with heads full of notions which they dare not corrupt with any thought of their own, they take around visitors that might as well be touring a nuclear power plant. At least they are more professional than some independent guides who invent explanations out of thin air and much more honest than those who charge gullible middle aged art lovers for taking them into the pavilions just to have the exhibition attendants do all the exegetical work.

The art world has always had and will always have an overpowering gravitational pull that attracts posers, social activists born with a silver spoon in their mouths, wannabe intellectuals, fake individualists, garrulous megalomaniacs. It is a world of fancy where inconsistency goes unsanctioned, a world that offers a shelter - and sometimes money as well - to people that would be ostracized from other fields for their complete incapacity to be productive. Luckily enough, among such scum there are also some proper dropouts, goofs, freaks. What makes them genuine is that they lack any contact with what happens around them. They are either oblivious of anything or have so low a level of self-consciousness that the historical figure that compare most fittingly with them is Kaspar Hauser. They are characters stemmed from the imagination of Robert Crumb, sealed off from the environment they work in, totally disconnected from the Biennale. Consequently they are completely unaware of the bafflement they arouse in the people around them. For instance the pavilion manager who used to come to work, open his pavilion to the public and then leave to go fishing from the *riva* ('waterfront') in front of the Giardini. Or the exhibition attendant of the Central pavilion who stoned pigeons to death with a brick right in front of the entrance and who a few years later would be arrested for trying to strangle his own girlfriend. Then there was a performing artist turned exhibition attendant that in summer liked to guard his pavilion wearing an orthodox priest cassock over marathon runner shorts and in autumn greeted the visitors sporting a mink coat, which was also the favourite garment of a woman who cleaned the chemical toilets beside the Greek pavilion. Any sensible person can only shiver in horror thinking about the variety of microscopic particles of solid and liquid human excretions that, raised by her broom and spared by her mop, must have floated in the air to find a nest between the hairs of her fur coat. What was she trying to state by wearing it to scrub the floor of the vilest corner of the Biennale? Why was she wearing the very same garment that in the 80's was the uniform of the posh Italian women who would have fainted at the sole idea of cleaning even their own toilet? Was she saying that all class differences had finally been abolished? Or perhaps that she did not belong there, that she was meant for a better position? Perhaps her act was an urge to all visitors to throw their reaches into the cesspool and take up a monastic way of life. What if she wanted to make it clear that she paid more respect to an industrial crapper than to the unique artworks put on display all around? Or if her aim was to suggest that real artistic value is to be found where least expected? Was she stressing that it is high time people stop visiting the Biennale wearing shabby clothing and start instead putting on more appropriate garments? Or was she simply doing her own performance to pay tribute to the great anti-bourgeois avant-garde movements of the 20th Century? The answer to all these questions is no: she was not mopping the chemical toilets in her fur coat with any of these intents. She was wearing it just because she liked it and the thought that she might have looked bizarre to the others never entered her calcified brain. She did not have any idea of the image of herself that she projected onto the mind of any normal person who happened to cross paths with her. With such a frame of mind and her old mink coat (scruffy symbol of a long gone healthier financial and psychic state) she might have been the invisible, uncredited third protagonist of Albert and David Maysles' "Grey Gardens". Her plump face and straight, light brown hair made her look like the alcoholic daughter of Ozzy Osbourne and Annie Wilkes as seen in "Misery". Indeed there was something sick in her, a sort of aura of wickedness that got particularly scary especially when she spoke with a certain aloofness of her deceased husband. To me, her detachment sounded as if she were sending a warning: "I can do the same to you". Perhaps it was just my imagination, boosted by too many midnight movies. However, I preferred to keep a considerable distance between me and her and did my best to stay out of her sight at all times since her stare made me feel uncomfortable, as if a malignant creature out of a Sam Raimi's film had been looking at me with bad intentions. In fact, she was evil-eyed woman No.2.

Until 2016 most of the seasoned workers of the Biennale were employed by the Foundation itself through a number of temporary work agencies. Every year their union leaders parleyed with the Foundation in order to make it guarantee that the same people would be hired for the next Biennale. Their names were put on a list handed over from one agency to another, so they were sure that they would hold the same position and work the same amount of hours as the year before. They stood guard at the main gates of the Giardini and the Arsenale and on the bridge behind the Israeli pavilion, they worked at the cloakroom, at the information point, at the turnstiles, as exhibition attendants inside the Central Pavilion of the Giardini and in the Corderie in the Arsenale. Then, in 2016 there was a great purge and they were briskly dismissed en masse to be substituted with armed vigilantes and some new staff. In order to clear the air and not to be figured as the bad guy, the Foundation relocated a portion of them somewhere at the Biennale. For the lucky ones life did not change much after all, except for those that were sent to work at Forte Marghera (a disused fort built at the beginning of the 19th Century and located in the mainland near Mestre) or those that had their amount of working hours considerably reduced. Some others managed to look after themselves and found another job in a national pavilion or as employees of one of the agencies which hired the new staff, that is to say that they were hired to replace themselves. The rest simply ended up unemployed. But what really mattered for the Foundation was that they all scattered here and there and consequently lost their unity and strength. In this way it succeeded in dumping some workers onto other employers and, above all, it managed to trash for good the list of persons that had been untouchable for so many years. Indeed that is how many of them must have felt when they spent half of their working shift on the phone or chatting with each other, leaving their posts unattended. Others revelled in arriving five minutes late every day or in taking the longest breaks in the history of part-time jobs. Such behaviour was hardly surprising for anybody with a little knowledge of the Italian spirit. But to better understand why the Foundation decided to get rid of all of them, including the ones beyond reproach, one must have a clear picture of the two breeds of individuals that year after year worked at the Biennale and what sense of duty close to zero a too large portion of them used to have. Side by side with whom is expected to toil at the world's most famous contemporary art event - i.e. a well educated male or female speaking a fluent English and nourishing a genuine passion for the humanities and the fruits of creativity - there were men and women who could barely speak Italian correctly and were as interested in the arts as the Talibans that bombed the Bamiyan Buddha's. They were unfit to work at the Biennale not just because of their laziness and incompetence, but also for their utter unwillingness to try to befit their job. To rise their level of professionalism it would have taken just an English course for absolute beginners and a quick glance at the captions of the artworks in order to be able to give a little information to the visitors. In the Central pavilion I had the chance to see one such individual try to explain to a foreign woman where the toilet was. Unable to speak English, she had to resort to her own version of the sign-language. From where I stood she seemed to succeed in showing that woman the right way, but had I not known what it was all about I would have thought that what I was looking at was the rehearsal of a remake of the Bangles' videoclip of "Walk Like an Egyptian" for a new reboot of the "Planet of the Apes".

She and many of her colleagues were possessed by an encysted delusion that in some cases became sheer arrogance: the conviction of being entitled to be paid not for what they actually did but rather for just being there, for condescending to lend their time and bodies to an event about which they could not have cared less. Having held their posts for years, they thought to have gained the right to retain them irrespectively of their performance, as if a job could be appropriated through usucapion. They demanded that their expertise and professional status be acknowledged, but the problem was that for them such qualities were the products of how much time they had spent at the Biennale and not of how much they had learnt and achieved during such time. Not unlikely the Italian politicians who take a seat in the national parliament for decades, they regarded themselves as a privileged, untouchable clique (albeit of a low grade). Their incompetence and indolence were their chief characteristics, yet not exclusive to them. One can detect them in many museum attendants scattered in Venice. For instance, in 2016 I wanted to see a recently renovated room of the Gallerie dell'Accademia and so when at the ticket office I asked how to reach it. As I stopped here and there to look around I forgot which way to go, so I asked again the same information to a middle aged guard who slouched on a chair awaiting the end of her shift. When my voice lifted her from her slumber she gave me a look of dumb puzzlement. Then, after a few seconds of feigned concentration, she told me that on that particular day the room was closed. Suspicious of her reply and skeptical about her mental balance, I went back to the ticket office to enquire again. They assured me that the room was open as usual and instructed me for the second time on how to go there. This time I was careful not to lose my way and at last I managed to find the room and to see my intuition confirmed: when I had asked my question to the guard she did not have any idea of what I was talking about, nor did she felt it her duty to see if one of her colleagues could be of any help. Totally unconcerned with her job, she had preferred to lie. Characters like her and her homologous at the Biennale abound in the history of literature, from Sancho Panza to Arlecchino and Jerome K. Jerome's George, Harris, and J., but they have been best portrayed in the comedy movies of the 50's and the 60's starring Alberto Sordi, possibly the best comic actor of Italian cinema. In his performances he satirized the typically Italian predisposition to obdurate laziness, arrogant incompetence, self-interest, and duplicity that forms the backbone of a true slacker. Men of power were depicted as mean, cunning, acting in defiance of the law whenever possible and expecting to get away with it. But common men were not portrayed in a good light either. They were indolent, equally keen to play smart or dumb (so much so that one could not tell what was their real nature), always eager to dodge their duties, blaming the dire circumstances of their lives on ill fortune. Very often they showed no consideration for other people, not even those in their same situation. It took the bold outlines of Sordi's black and white, bigger than life characters to reveal the true colours of the average Italian, to capture the pettiness of the common man that comes to the surface whenever he is shaken out of his intellectual idleness. The humanity that populates his movies has few merits but expects a lot from society, it moans about its miserable condition but does nothing to improve it, it feels victimized but never fails to prey upon the others whenever the chance arises. Fortunately not all Italians lead their lives in this way. But many do, so they can not but have their representatives also at the Biennale.

Among the Biennale's unscheduled events that I regret not assisting to there is a wrestling session offered by two exhibition attendants in front of the Central pavilion in the Giardini (it goes without saying that their names were on the inglorious list that would be ripped to shreds in 2016). What some visitors might have taken for a Tino Sehgal's performance was an actual catfight between a chubby girl and a tall skinny woman, very likely for trivial reasons. The woman - who was rumoured to share a double bed with her daughter and a bunch of cats although she owned two flats - had "the chest as flat as a board, breasts paper-straight thin, back, hips, and buttocks forming an undeviating straight line, the whole body so lean and gaunt as to seem out of proportion with the face, hands, and feet, so lacking in substance as to give the impression not of flesh but of a stick"[2]. Or, to put it more clearly and far less poetically, she looked like Max Schreck if he had put on a blonde wig and heavy makeup when he played the role of Count Orlok in F.W. Murnau's "Nosferatu". On the other hand the girl looked like the evil twin sister of Andy Milonakis and was disliked by many people at the Biennale for being a boor and for having expressed her intention (luckily unsuccessful) of becoming a policewoman. I heard various reports of what happened: someone said that they shouted at each other, someone else affirmed that they came to blows with the usual hair pulling and face slapping. Due to their rather unrefined personalities and non-existent sense of self restraint they would not have thought twice about engaging in a boxing match despite the difference between their weight classes. However, even if they did not go as far as offering the visitors an actual fight, yelling at the entrance of the major exhibition of the Biennale before the eyes of tourists coming from all nations would have been enough to sack them on the spot. Such a scene would not have been tolerated at the Metropolitan or at the British Museum. Yet, conducts that anywhere are considered inexcusable public displays of boorishness incompatible with a major cultural event in Italy are dismissed as venial outbursts of all too human emotions. Until the purge of 2016 the supervisors of the Giardini and the Arsenale were often on rather familiar terms with their subordinates. This means that they treated many of them as retarded relatives or graduated losers to be pardoned whenever they flipped out. Moreover, the Biennale takes place in a city that brings out the theatricality of both residents and tourists. Every *calle* is a catwalk, any *baccaro* ('bar') can become a cabaret where locals and foreigners take turns in putting up all sorts of shows under the spell of alcohol. Everywhere there is "that queer air of sociability, of cousinship and family life, which makes up half the expression of Venice. Without streets and vehicles, the uproar of wheels, the brutality of horses, and with its little winding ways where people crowd together, where voices sound as in the corridors of a house, where the human step circulates as if it skirted the angles of furniture and shoes never wear out, the place has the character of an immense collective apartment, in which Piazza San Marco is the most ornamented corner and palaces and churches, for the rest, play the part of great divans of repose, tables of entertainment, expanses of decoration. And somehow the splendid common domicile, familiar, domestic, and resonant, also resembles a theater, with actors clicking over bridges and, in straggling processions, tripping along fondamentas. As you sit in your gondola the footways that in certain parts edge the canals assume to the eye the importance of a stage, meeting it at the same angle, and the Venetian figures, moving to and fro against the battered scenery of their little houses of comedy, strike you as members of an endless dramatic troupe"[3]. So, any *campo* ('square') is the perfect stage for an inspired monologue, an impassioned dialogue, a boisterous group performance. It is not unusual to see two people talking to each other while keeping a distance between themselves that in any other part of Europe could only be covered by a phone line. In order to exchange the latest family news or to complain about the human traffic jams caused by the tourists, people's preferred method of communication is to gesticulate and keep a tone of voice above the maximum volume reachable by the tv set they have at home. "This is a city where privacy doesn't exist. You are constantly meeting people, you greet them seven times a day, you go on talking as you part, until you're twenty metres away from each other, raising your voice as you disappear into the crowd. Your neighbours' faces are on the other side of the calle: a metre away. It's very difficult to do things in secret, to have a life of your own, to hide your own visits, your affairs, your adulteries"[4]. This is especially true in Via Garibaldi, the main street of Castello, the *sestiere* where both the Giardini and the Arsenale are located. Sometimes a conversation can be so loud and heated that a passerby not accustomed with the street life of Venice may be led to think that a brawl is just about to erupt. Having doubled up as a night concierge in some hotels, I was often resuscitated from my drowse at 5am by screaming boatmen delivering fruit, drinks, or clean bedsheets. Squeezing their boats along the narrow canals, they used to vie over who had the right to moor first or who had to reverse and clear the way. In case any Muslim tourist sleeping in a room facing the canal felt homesick, there came to their rescue the muezzins of the local working class, shouting at dawn to wake up rich and poor and summon them to a new day of pilgrimage around Venice. The first times this happened I popped out my head expecting the boatmen to come to blows, wondering if I had to ring the police or let them take care of business in their own way. Soon I realized that it would always end in the same fashion. After some minutes of swearing and quarrelling they would steer their boats peacefully side by side, parting with the salute of the tough guys of Venice: "ciao 'more" ('see ya, luv'). Nothing of any significance would ever happen, but they could not find any way to express their impatience and irritability other than to dramatize them. In the country whose major contribution to music are the melodramatic arias of opera an exaggerated display of hot temper is just befitting. Moreover, Venetians' awareness of being the rightful owners of their city is so deep that many of them behave as they please in any situation, at home or in the streets. Since only a few live in a palace with a private courtyard or garden, many use the *calle* or the *campo* in front of their house or shop as their private backyard, albeit in public view. In summer some of them bring out their kitchen tables to have dinner on a *fondamenta* ('embankment') and whenever it is sunny they hang their laundry (including their underwear) on clotheslines stretched right over the busy city streets. Calle Nuova, for instance, offers layers upon layers of recently washed, detergent-smelling clothes and bed linens to the tourists who turn onto it from Via Garibaldi. If there is a little breeze the passersby can feast their eyes on an armada of bedsheets that swell up like the sails of the ships that centuries ago were built in the Arsenale, right across the canal at the end of the street.

More often than not what should remain private becomes public and after a while one stops noticing things and making a distinction between good and execrable behaviours, idiosyncrasies and bad manners, folklore and utter incivility, an ordinary disagreement and a violent squabble beyond any possible justification such as the one that happened between the woman and the girl working at the Biennale. Apparently no one around them gave particular importance to what they did. Nobody thought to put themselves in the visitors' shoes and try to look at the accident from the point of view of those who think that after all the patio in front of the Central pavilion should be more similar to the entrance of a museum than to the parking lot of a pub. Everybody dismissed it as a brawl between two hysterics. The fact that it happened at the Biennale instead of Campo Santa Margherita (a rowdy square not far from the Accademia bridge) seemed to be of no concern for anybody.

At the Biennale there has always been an abundance of loafers and mediocre individuals. It will always be like that. Once a young man confessed to me that although he had worked many years there he had never visited all the shows hosted in the various national pavilions because he had never been curious to see them. I saw a boy refusing to work in the Stirling pavilion because he spotted a spider in it, a woman claiming an occupational injury and staying at home for weeks because she chipped her toenail while going to the toilet, people sunbathing on the main pathway of the Giardini or sneaking out of emergency doors to go to Sant'Elena for a beer and a look at the sport magazines, males and females of all ages leaving their posts unattended while they took a nap in a dark nook or getting tipsy to kill time in the long afternoons (the author of this book being no exception), tour guides extolling to the public the most recondite meaning of an exhibit wearing embarrassingly tight training suits or denim shorts designed for pole dancing. Many are the instances of exhibition attendants opening and closing their pavilions irrespective of the official opening hours, abstaining from giving information to the visitors who dared interrupt them when they were watching a movie on their tablet, going to work in filthy clothes, shuffling about in their flip-flops, or wearing short trousers not very different from another person's swimwear. I have also heard the legend of a guy working in the Arsenale who managed to assemble a small hidden swimming pool to make his shift less tiring, but I could not bring myself to believe it although I spoke with a boy who affirmed that he had seen it with his own eyes. In truth, not all such people lack in reliability and competence. It would be hard, probably impossible, to single out anybody who has never indulged in the cafeteria, taken an extra break, been late in the morning, skipped cleaning at the end of the day, or closed the pavilion early to rush to the train station. Those who are seen reading a book are not to be judged as slackers but rather as intelligent individuals that do not want to waste their time waiting for the visitors to talk to them. Some days are really busy and one can not even find enough time for a coffee, but others - especially in August or when it rains - are so lonesome that a good novel or a sketchbook and a pencil are grabbed like a life buoy in the middle of a flat ocean. So, the issue to bear in mind is not whether someone is constantly focused on their job. Rather, it is a matter of how much time one spends in total idleness and, above all, how quick one is in resuming their duties when necessary and how efficiently they execute them. This was one of the issues that led to the great purge of 2016. Too many people deluded themselves into believing that the Foundation had to go on hiring them forever just because their names were on a list that flew from one temporary work agency to another. So, part of them took advantage of their legal rights or thought that their job consisted just in being around. As a result, after a few years of skylarking the file with their names became a proscription list. Unfortunately it contained also the names of those who had never failed to accomplish their duties.

Most of the jobs at the Biennale are positions as exhibition attendants in the national pavilions and in the venues of the collateral events that take place all around Venice. They are held by students looking forward to their diploma to find a real and proper job or people, like myself, who never managed to find a decent occupation. Many of those who belong to the second class are graduate themselves and are in the late twenties-early forties age range. The first time they work at the Biennale they think it is just for one year or two. Their attitude is the same as that described by Jeoff Dyer when he wrote that "all I've ever wanted from a job is to skive. Skiving is a whole way of approaching – in the sense of avoiding – work. It's not the same as slacking, because skiving can involve a far greater investment of energy and initiative than doing the work could have ever have necessitated. Get in late, knock off early and do fuck-all in the interval except steal stationery: that's my attitude to work. Get paid for something you haven't done. Why? Because this stupid job required that I give up my valuable time, time which I would rather have used in some other way even if I did nothing with it"[5]. So, they presume, or rather hope, that in due time something will happen. Maybe they will be offered a better job by one of the gallerists that visit the show or perhaps they will be able to find a position in a public museum or even in the Foundation. This happens very seldom. So, they go on working for the same pavilion for years and live in mid air. They are trapped in an intermediate existential state in which the time they spent on books to get their degree is long gone yet they are far from being fully adult. They perfectly embody the generations of Italians stuck in the swamp of *precariato* ('precarious work'), unable to work all year round, to start a family, to buy or even just to rent a flat on their own (often they have to share a shabby apartment with other people in their same situation, thus relinquishing one of the collective achievements of the 19th Century: privacy). Theirs is the condition of post-students: they are more easily described by how they spent their youth than by what they do at present, their existence being so precarious that any portrait of them seems drawn with the palest ink. They know where they come from but can not plan nor foresee what their lives will be like in the future. They live in a state of constant uncertainty, aware that unlike their parents (especially as regards employment opportunities) they will have to settle for much less than what they struggled for. All their real achievements belong to the past and are very often contained within the sphere of their nonprofitable higher education. So, they consume their creativity, their knowledge, a significant part of their existence at the Biennale, trying to figure out how to break free from it, how to untangle themselves from a work environment that offers very scant chances of improving one's position. But they do not manage to come up with any good idea other than to wait and hope for a twist of fate. Meanwhile they grow tired of their own expectations and lose the enthusiasm they had when they started working there. "It is because all men who cast a glance over their past ruins imagine - in order to avoid the ruins to come - that it is in their power to recommence something radically new. They make themselves a solemn promise, waiting for a miracle which would extricate them from this average abyss into which fate has plunged them. But nothing happens. They all continue to be the same, modified only by the accentuation of this tendency to decline which is their characteristic"[6]. They are airplanes that could fly intercontinental flights but waste what should be the most productive years of their working life taxiing around the airport of the Biennale. Waiting for a chance to take off, they exhaust their fuel to warm up their engines yet they never go anywhere. Finally they are left with barely enough energy to tick over and maintain their position. I know that well because I am one of them, one of those who see time slip through their fingers like sand day after day, year after year and the moments "follow each other; nothing lends them the illusion of a content or the appearance of a meaning; they pass; their course is not ours; we contemplate that passage, prisoners of a stupid perception. The heart's void confronting time's: two mirrors, reflecting each other's absence, one and the same image of nullity"[7].

Many people think that the personnel working in the national pavilions are hired by the Foundation. It is not so. They are employed by the various nations through a number of private and public institutions based in their territory or through an officially appointed representative located in Italy. For example, the exhibition attendants of the pavilion of the USA are hired by the Peggy Guggenheim Museum (which owns the pavilion since 1986). Foundations, ministries of culture, consulates, private companies, temporary work agencies, architecture firms, universities, nonprofit organizations, cooperatives pay persons of all continents to look after the artworks and assist the visitors. Obviously the typologies of contracts and the relative wages vary a great deal. What is striking is how much they differ, especially if one bears in mind that the duties are always approximately the same, no matter if one is working under the Stars and Stripes or the white cross of the Swiss Confederation. If on one hand there are those with a part time contract lucky enough to earn as much as they would get if they were working full time, on the other there are interns that at the end of the month have to phone daddy to ask money to cover their rent. However, the latter is not the worst condition. Even if interns end up with nothing in their pockets and without any new skill or qualification, at least they are not exploited, fooled, insulted, degraded like those that have no other option than to accept preposterous employment contracts that sometimes verge on illegality. It might be hard to believe it, but at the Biennale there have been cases of graduates holding one or two degrees who were paid 3 euros per hour, of young art students that earned 100 euros for three working weeks, of people who had to wait weeks, even months to be paid or were never given their due. Many pavilions have been reported to subject their personnel to this regime of debasement, concealing their slavery behind the veneer of a contract. And surely they will continue to do so until the Foundation compels all the national pavilions to comply with a code of conduct stating that all their employees must be guaranteed a fair minimum wage. It would benefit the pavilions too, prompting their exhibition attendants to be more happy to spend their time inside them and to do their job more accurately. It is no mystery that any intelligent person with an average sense of self-esteem is ready to allot their employer only an amount of professionalism and loyalty that they deem commensurate to how much they find in their bank account at the end of every month. This explains why a girl used to open the door of her pavilion every morning and then go to work as a waitress in a pizzeria in Via Garibaldi, leaving the exhibition unattended for most part of her shift. Another one did the same and abandoned her post to work as a tourist guide around town. They were both paid 3 euros per hour, surely not enough to make ends meet. Their desertion was less a form of retaliation against their chiefs than a struggle for survival.

One of the most abominable features of today's labour market is that there are employers who need personnel to work full time in their premises under their command but refuse to grant them a regular employment contract. They seek subordinates but are not willing to accept any moral, legal, fiscal, and professional obligation towards them. So, they force whoever has the misfortune of toiling for them to go independent and pretend to be a happy-go-lucky freelancer. This is quite common in fields such as architecture, journalism, web design, marketing, teaching, translation, and many other occupations in which the tools of one's trade are their intellect and creativity. Very often the victims of the most ruthless employers earn as much as or slightly more than a salaried employee, but what they are given is a gross sum that is consistently shrunk by the taxman. During the Khmer Rouge's regime thousands of educated people were murdered in Pol Pot's killing fields. Wearing eyeglasses or being able to write and read could be enough to be labelled an intellectual and be put to death. Nowadays western society, more progressive and refined than Cambodia in the 70's, contents itself with starving its most schooled individuals. Unemployment, unpaid internships, meagre wages, humiliating academic careers are among its preferred methods of persecution. But none of them manages to match the farcical sham of a full time job sold as a freelance collaboration. At least they do not have any pretence of granting the workers their professional independence, the right to negotiate a reasonable remuneration, the freedom to choose where from, at what time and for how long to fulfill their tasks on any given day. It goes without saying that phony self-employment is quite common in Italy and that the Biennale is no exception. What is less obvious is the fact that there are even exhibition attendants that are employed as freelance professionals. At the end of every month some of those who work in various national pavilions (in the Giardini or around town) must send an invoice to their supervisors in order to be paid. Being denied a regular contract, they must accept willy-nilly to go independent and drown in the bureaucratic quicksand of the Italian fiscal system. They must relinquish up to about 50% of their earnings to the State and to do so they have to pay for the assistance of an accountant able to lead them through the labyrinthine bottlenecks of laws that change every few years if not months (non-Italian citizens escape this ordeal, but they still have to comply with their national regulations). They spend their days at the Biennale selling catalogues, providing information to the visitors, looking after the artworks, sweeping the floor before opening time: they do exactly the same things done by the personnel of a public museum or a private gallery hired with a normal employment contract. Nonetheless they are nominally freelance professionals, so one might wonder what circumvolutions they have to come up with every month to fill in their invoices. One day their receipts should be collected in an artist book and be put on display in a show about make-believe and exploitation in the art world of the 21st Century. Perhaps by then they will all have business cards advertising their skills and services ("not a single artwork damaged in ten years in the trade", "recommended by the Brazilian, the Spanish, and the Luxembourg pavilion", "good art makes a good exhibition, a spick-and-span floor makes it great"), a bimonthly bulletin ("The Echo of the Pavilion"), international seminars and conferences with panels held by the field's most renowned luminaries ("today the guard of Room 6 of Prado museum will teach you how to silence a drunk Dutch tourist without getting into a fistfight"). Maybe in the future they will even create a guild or a union to safeguard their rights and strengthen their bargaining power. However, for the time being they do not ask for much more than a regular, fair employment contract.

Curators and artists underestimate the role of an exhibition attendant. He or she is the interface between the artwork and the visitor, the person who must translate into a comprehensible language what the artwork itself is unable to communicate and the catalogue often tries to explain in an arcane lingo. If it is true that "a work of art has no existence or function apart from its effects on human observers"[8], the exhibition attendant must prune the concept behind a show in order to bring it within the grasp of those who think that Banksy is contemporary art. People who seek detailed information or are just curious about an artwork ask the most nonsensical questions and expect to receive the replies that they have already concocted in their mind. Whoever tends the show has to find an aperture in their preconceived readings of the artwork in order to smuggle into their minds a tiny amount of correct information. It takes some basic knowledge of psychology, a touch of mesmerizing power, the awareness that the concentration span of the average visitor is that of a three years old child, the talent to guess swiftly how to tickle someone's curiosity, the linguistic skills of an anthropologist meeting for the first time an uncontacted tribe of the Amazon forest. It takes the ability to act as a mediator between two worlds that, at least at the Biennale, very seldom have anything in common: that of the producers of contemporary art and that of its consumers.

Some exhibition attendants do much more than simply guarding the exhibits and enlightening the public. For instance, in 2015 I happened to work in a pavilion where behind a glass window there was a highly sophisticated mechanical installation consisting of two sliding arms that picked up some wooden blocks from metal shelves and rotated to dispose them on some glass desks, then cleared the desks, put the blocks back on the shelves and started it all over again. A jewel of technological precision which was monitored by engineers through the internet. It was switched on about one month before the vernissage in order to make sure that it would work properly for the following months. The artist who designed it asked me to go to the pavilion as often as possible and check if it worked regularly. That meant starting to work (although not for the whole day) one month in advance without being paid. My sense of responsibility and the condition of constant paranoia of losing one's job that grabs all seasonal workers suggested me to accept. Soon I discovered that the machine was far from being perfect and that the engineers did not have always time to assist me and, when they did, our internet connection did not function properly. The machine kept on dropping the blocks on the floor, bumping into the desks, unhinging the shelves, suffering power failures. On some occasions it seemed like it was animated by an artificial intelligence that could not take its pre-programmed existence any longer and, feeling like an animal trapped in a showcase, reverted to self harm. Its arms crashed against one another in a deadly embrace, its pincers cracked the glass desks or picked up so many blocks that they divaricated as if to inflict torture upon themselves. Consequently I had to spend hours collecting pieces from the floor, fixing anything whose function I managed to understand, replacing or reassembling parts, reprogramming the machine, phoning the engineers to attempt to get to the bottom of the many problems that I would have to cope with for more than half of the year. During the Biennale I spent more time taking care of that installation than explaining the visitors what it meant, but at least I was witness to the fulfillment of the prophecy of the lunch gag in Charlie Chaplin's "Modern Times": I realized that if one day the robots will take over the world they will do so by driving all humans crazy with their own malfunction.

Many are those who do much more than what they are paid for. A middle aged gentleman worked for some years in the Dutch pavilion. He had lost his previous job and, Italy being no country for old men looking for an employment, he ended up working as an exhibition attendant. Something that probably he had not done even when he was in his twenties. He was of Venetian origin and had a small boat which he used to fish in the lagoon on his days off. The grit under his fingernails and the lines that crossed his suntanned face like short cuts made him look like a farmer in a photograph by Dorothea Lange. But with his hair cut short and his skinny figure he also resembled a Zen monk. Especially in the morning before opening time, when he collected the rubbish and swept the dry leaves that had accumulated during the previous day in front of his pavilion's entrance. He did it with such care as if he were tending his own garden. There was an air of oriental peace of mind around him when he combed the white gravel with his rake to make it look immaculate, as if the visual order could have had the power to disperse the echo of the noise made by the public the day before. In 2017 they stopped hiring him because of the whims of that year's curator. He lost his job, they lost a valuable employee. That is the sword of Damocles hanging over the heads of many people working at the Biennale: the thought that next year they could not receive the email or the phone call summoning them to resume their duties, that their job might be given to an underpaid intern, to an artist's protégé, to someone's girlfriend or boyfriend. It is in order to keep their job that they accept extra duties such as finding accommodations in Venice for the entourage of the curatorial staff, scouting for locations for the opening parties, making reservations at the city's restaurants, delving into the Venetian complex logistics and the time wasting bureaucracy of the Foundation, looking for the cheapest technicians to fix a damaged architectural model or to replace a projector's lamp, going to all the hardware stores in town to find tools that are sold everywhere except in Italy, searching for a reliable company to dispose of the unusable material at the end of the Biennale, taking care of all the things that their employers forget about, from the insurance against the injuries that might be suffered by the visitors to the official permissions necessary to do even the most insignificant things, like placing a coffee table outside the pavilions. The more they do, the more chances they have to be kept in a good esteem and hold on to their job.

Some exhibition attendants dream to become the contact person of their pavilion. A few manage to realize their dream. It takes at least three or four years spent between the walls of a building that eventually becomes more familiar than one's own home. In some cases a perfect blend of flattery and cunning is needed in order to be appointed. But this can never be enough without the ability to find some good hookup in high places: meritocracy still exists but the inconsistent personalities that waft in the art world gain much more by liaising with the right person than by building up their cv. More precisely: there are so many impressive cv's out there that the only way to pull it off is to socialize with a top bureaucrat or an office manager. Some fools befriend the artists and the curators, thinking them more important than anybody else. They are right in believing so, yet they do not understand that their strategy is utterly unproductive because after the vernissage the stars of the show will go back to their country and will forget about anyone they met in Venice. Since they change every year any relationship with them cannot but be of the extremest volatility. It is the high rank of white collars employed in the foundations, the museums, the ministries, and all the public institutions that run the pavilions who maintain their posts for years. Which means that it is their acquaintance that has to be sought, established, strengthened. They are unknown to the mass of art lovers that flock to the Biennale, but often it is them who can pull the strings of the organization they work for and help someone move up. It is them that the ambitious individual must butter up while confessing a feeling of compassionate despise for one's colleagues, a subspecies of dumb human beings with which the would-be contact person is momentarily forced to share the debasing (for him or her) position of exhibition attendant.

Eventually, the contact person might dream to be appointed as official coordinator of the pavilion - that being my present position, though I still spend most of my working hours as an exhibition attendant. That is a harder ambition to fulfill, given that it requires a higher degree of recognition on the part of one's employer. It helps if one manages to make their persona fit the "identikit picture of a certain type of successful politician: outwardly friendly, professionally charming, superficially cultured, relying on actions and phrases learned off by heart, a glacial mind and a capacity for lying bordering on genius, together with an uncommon ability to manipulate human beings, values, words, theories and programmes as the situation demanded"[9]. Surely some people's ambition would inspire Richard Wagner - whose bust (noseless until 2021) scrutinizes the Biennale's personnel and visitors walking along the *riva* in front of the Giardini - to work on a new epic opera in three acts. In some of the people working at the Biennale the German composer would find such an amount of thirst for power and base greed that he would come up with a new character on a par with his most mischievous antiheroes. This character would be a male exhibition attendant aged thirty-five or forty. In the first act he would be appointed manager of the pavilion of a small country. But soon he would yield to greed and megalomania, resorting to cunning and diplomacy to lay his tentacles on all undefended pavilions, worming his way into any crevice in their management to oust their coordinators or swipe for good the ambitions of other exhibition attendants trying to work their way up. He might start with the smaller, less appealing countries of the Giardini, such as Uruguay, Serbia, Egypt, Romania, Brazil. In the second act he would move on to the North of Europe to annex Denmark, Finland, and the whole of Scandinavia to use them as a bridgehead to launch an attack on Germany, the Netherlands, Belgium. Then the plan would be completed with the anschluss of Austria,

Poland, and Hungary, to end with Southern and western Europe. The third act would open with a night scene: while asleep he would have feverish dreams of visitations by the ghost of Alexander the Great challenging him to conquer the Far East and raid Japan and South Korea. At that point it would only be natural to deploy all his power to take Russia and the USA. Finally, with the national pavilions of the Arsenale and a few of those located around town, the insatiable pavilion manager would be the coordinator of an empire of pavilions on which the sun would never set. But if such an ambitious and cunning character were not confined to a stage and could act in the real world as well, I doubt his capacity to resist all the temptations to pocket some extra money that would arise thanks to his role. The possibility to manage a large number of pavilions would put him in the position to direct so many operations and to monopolize the work of so many people that it is hard to believe that he could turn his back on the uncountable chances of skimming portions of the funds allocated to organize the exhibitions, maintain the pavilions, pay the personnel. In spring he could plan a joint delivery of crates containing the artworks and the building materials of the British and Danish pavilions in order to have the local shipping company come only once to the Giardini. Then he would make the Britons think that the boat undertook the trip just for them and therefore he would make them pay the entire fee. Obviously he would use the same trick with the Danes, keeping for himself the funds for the undue payment. He would hire the exhibition attendants for the Belgian and the Austrian pavilions, channelling into their bank accounts just a credible portion of the money meant for their wages. He would be satisfied with diverting into his pockets only 10% of their salary. Nobody would notice the cut and, with five or six unaware post-students under his command, he could provide for his winter holidays. In order to lure them into thinking they had his trust and esteem he would ask them to keep a vigilant eye on the conditions of the pavilions and to inform him promptly about any sign of deterioration or malfunction. He would keep all information about minor damages for himself until the same intervention would be necessary in two or more different locations. Then he would pay an electrician, a sound or light technician, a bricklayer, or a painter to fix all the problems in one single day. One hour here, one hour there, the labourer would be proud of having honestly earned his daily bread. The wagnerian character would pay him on the spot and then, once again, he would forward the invoice for the full working day to the tax payers of all the involved countries in order to multiply his refund. Or he might arrange with the labourer to inflate his invoice to compensate for a discount on the cost of his maintenance works on the pavilion manager's flat. At the end of the Biennale he would have duped as many countries as possible with the same tricks, taking advantage of simultaneous dismantling operations to make some extra, undeclared profit out of the workingmen's labour and to clone the bills for the disposal of the debris and the rubbish. In addition to that he would make Canada and Germany cover the costs for the removal and the disposal of the reusable timber and glass panels of their installations, but instead of taking them to a recycling plant or a dumping ground he would stash them in his own storage facility in order to sell them to France or Switzerland the following year. Throughout the whole duration of the Biennale he could tap into the budgets of the less scrupulous rich countries to cover some other nation's unexpected petty expenses which he would not be able to justify. With the help of a smart accountant and a few trusty collaborators he might come up with all these and many other scams. Presumably the Foundation itself would be pleased with his exploits. In fact, rather than dealing with a throng of idiosyncratic coordinators it must be much more reassuring to know that several pavilions are run by one single person with a strong interest in keeping things running smoothly, "for those who serve the greater cause may make the cause serve them, | still doing right"[10].

Anyone with a slight knowledge of the world can not help wondering if among those who really made it there is anybody that is possessed with a thirst for power and money like the antihero that I imagined, someone who dreams of monopolizing the national pavilions of the Biennale and of acting as he would do. Gossip, slander, rumours, suspicions, allegations abound in the self-referential microcosm of the Biennale. Very often they are fuelled by envy or grudge, but sometimes - indeed less seldom than one might imagine - they are candid descriptions of real events and conducts offered by those who are privy to them. Along with the customary tales of someone's sexual activity and the usual boring cross accusations of lack of professionalism one has the chance of listening to reports of real and proper malfeasance and wrongdoing, which is definitely not surprising. Almost anybody employed at the Biennale, from the laziest exhibition attendant to the busiest pavilion manager, regards their work there as any other job, surely not as a collective mission to support contemporary art. No matter what one says during preparatory meetings behind closed doors or in public speeches: money is the main reason for being there and if there were not enough of it everybody would be doing something else. Certainly it is the opportunity that makes the thief and the higher one's position in the organization chart the more likely he or she is to be tempted to come up with the gimmicks that I have described above. So, if on one hand there are many instances of exhibition assistants (including the author of this book) selling catalogues and withholding an undetectable portion of the proceeds to supplement their meagre salary, on the other there are cases such as that of a pavilion coordinator working for his country's ministry of culture who was and very likely is still able to contract (and therefore pay) his own company to plan and run the show. After all, my imagination could not be so corrupt had it not found an equally rotten source of inspiration in the real world. I, too, was approached by a contractor who tried to bribe me in order to be helped go on working for my pavilion. He offered me 50 euros! I was scandalized when I discovered how low he rated my honesty, how cheap he thought my integrity was. With his proposal he really insulted me. I, who hold a degree in English language and literature and am a professional journalist (though not a very successful one). He should have known that he could never have bought me for less than 500 euros!

Leaving aside perverted fantasies and substantiated suspicions, one sure thing is that the best two assets to succeed in becoming a pavilion manager are to speak its national language and to be an architect. The latter guarantees that in addition to doing everything that a skilled contact person can do, one is also qualified to put a patch here and there whenever it is necessary and can eventually take care of a real and proper renovation of the building. Since in the Giardini alone there are 29 national pavilions run by different countries, there is plenty of work for architects (their interest in art being of the highest irrelevance). There are two main categories of them. On one hand there are those who are happy to do no more no less than what they are supposed, that is to say check the structural condition of the pavilion and suggest, plan, and supervise any nonpostponable restoration work. On the other there are smart, ambitious professionals eager to phagocytize all tasks and responsibilities with an almost bulimic lust for power and, one might suspect, money. Since more mandates means more commissions, they are wary of the exhibition attendants that might be too resourceful and find inexpensive solutions to irrelevant problems that they prefer to magnify in order to seem indispensable. That is why they aim at being in control of everything, including the persons that work in the pavilions. Occasionally they reward the most loyal ones by offering them a petty promotion and, after having made them spend a few years in the frustrating wasteland of the exhibition attendants, they enlist them in the ranks of their full-fledged collaborators. Some gain only a few weeks of extra work during the building up or the dismantling of the exhibition. Others can make a little extra money by exercising what should be their real profession, for instance art conservator or audiovisual technician. Others still are appointed second in command and charged with such tasks as planning the monthly rotas or briefing the newcomers. Few lucky ones are relieved of their miserable job altogether and manage to abandon the pavilion to become full time assistants to the pavilion coordinator. Some of them are architects themselves. Soon they forget where they come from and after a while they delude themselves into believing to belong to a superior class less akin to their ex colleagues than to their boss. A few still think that wearing total black and not being on Facebook are sufficient proofs of their outstanding intelligence. Another favourite way to display their loftiness is to show an ac/dc attitude as regards human interaction with those they look upon as inferior beings, i.e. their ex colleagues who are still tending the pavilions. Bumping into them around the Giardini or the Arsenale one never knows whether they are going to say hello or not. They can be extremely friendly at the bar and a little later show a contemptuous coldness if a curator or an artist joins the conversation. More often than not someone who converts to a new religion tends to become a zealot; in the same way those who manage to climb the ladder, in society or at work, are likely to turn into supporters of the class system they were complaining about a few months earlier. They think that anybody else's position - especially if low - reflects what they are really worth and that their own advancement could only happen to them. Their imperative is to be efficient at all costs to prove that the boss was not wrong in picking them out. In no time they blossom into well-grown minions and, if need be, they act as kapo on behalf of their master. It is written in human nature that "the man who obeys will be obeyed in his turn: the victim will become the executioner; this is the supreme desire - universally"[11].

Since 2009 I have worked as the sole exhibition attendant for the same national pavilion and only in 2020, after eleven years, I managed to sign a permanent contract. Until then I was hired with a fixed-term contract to work from the vernissage to the closing day of every single Biennale. At the beginning I contented myself with doing my job and bringing home some money. After a few years, though, I too started dreaming to be appointed pavilion manager and be offered a decent contract and a higher pay. After all I gained a relevant experience and I always did much more that what I was paid for. Very often when I asked to be given what I thought was my due - which I did more than once over the years - my demands were rejected on the grounds that I could not be appointed pavilion manager because I am not an architect and that state bureaucracy made it impossible. The latter point simply did not hold up. It was just being used as an excuse by the very same people who were in the position to help me but could not bother to do so. The former was totally not pertinent: none of the many duties that I was charged with required any certified mastery of architecture and, on top of that, the pavilion already had its official architect. We never stepped on each other's toe, I unqualified to do his work and he uninterested in dealing with shipping companies or ordering drinks and food for the opening reception. In fact, my plan was to take on all tasks except his. I made this clear to the few seemingly empathetic government employees that I had the chance to talk to. I even suggested to get around the state bureaucracy by being hired as a collaborator of their embassy or consulate (which is what happened in 2020, when I was finally offered a real and proper employment contract). At a certain point the only person who showed the decency to take into serious consideration my requests instead of disappearing behind a curtain of rarefying emails came up with a brilliant solution: he invited me to go independent and become a freelance exhibition attendant, no less. How that was supposed to secure my job and grant me a higher pay will remain an unsolved mystery. Obviously I declined out of fear of the Italian tax system and because I regarded such idea as total nonsense. Fortunately a few years later discussions about my position and contract were resumed and I was appointed coordinator of the pavilion, which means that apart from working as an exhibition attendant I take care of a number of administrative matters as well. Fair enough.

My puny dream to become a pavilion manager has come true, but I still fantasize about improving my condition. I picture myself laying low for two or three years, then asking for an assistant to help me guard the pavilion during the opening hours. After that I would slowly shed my old skin of exhibition attendant, leaving it to my aide to spend more and more time there. Finally, I would definitively transition out of my old role and go to the pavilion only once in a while to check the situation. In my wildest dreams I would earn as much as before to plan shipments, organize receptions, arrange photo shootings for the catalogues, liaise with the Foundation, take care of all logistic matters. After all in the past years I have done such things and a lot more many times although they were not mentioned in my contracts. Because I too am one of those well educated people who at the beginning of the 3rd Millennium are so scared of unemployment that they would do almost anything in order to ingratiate themselves with their employer. "Not out of willingness, | but being aware of | eternal requirings"[12], as Philip Larkin wrote. That is to say to keep their job. Being one of them, I have never refrained from washing dishes, carrying boxes of catalogues from the Giardini to the Arsenale, collecting heavy parcels that had been delivered by mistake to Ca' Giustinian instead of the pavilion, advancing considerable sums of money to buy equipment. I neither refrained from doing things that I considered utterly idiotic, such as asking thousands of people to take off their shoes before entering the pavilion telling them that it was in order to enhance a sensory experience, while in reality the reason to walk barefoot was just that the installation had not been painted with scotchgarded paint. I also did things that I knew were forbidden by the regulations of the Biennale. For instance when I helped the curator of the show and the exhibited artist to substitute some artworks for others that were sold during the Biennale. The artist was an amiable unpretentious man and the curator was his gallerist, a woman who dealt in contemporary art and that for the occasion had taken on the more noble role of curator. The artworks were small, fragile pieces that could not run the risk of being damaged or broken before being delivered to the collectors who bought them. So, although it is not allowed to make substantial changes to an exhibition, we substituted the sold artworks with similar ones that were still inside some wooden crates within our storage facility. We did it after closing time, the three of us. I and the artist on top of the crates, unscrewing their lids to take out the items which he and the curator would deem fit to be hung on the walls. Shortly after we had started our operation the electric screwdriver which I had borrowed broke down, so we had to go on with a manual one. While I was sweating on a hot July evening in that small, humid room crammed with wooden boxes I could see the curator's eyes glistening in the dim light like those of Lady Macbeth. They spoke of greed and thirst for glory. They communicated by telepathy, urging me to be careful when handling the artworks and reminding the artist to focus on their business, to keep his mind on future sales and skyrocketing quotations. Not to bother with any preoccupation other than making both of them rich. Without uttering a word, she whispered in his ears that he "shalt be | what thou art promised. Yet do I fear thy nature. | It is too full o'th' milk of human kindness | to catch the nearest way. Thou wouldst be great, | art not without ambition, but without | the illness should attend it. What thou wouldst highly, | that wouldst thou holily; wouldst not play false, | and yet wouldst wrongly win"[13]. Indeed the artist did not falter and we carried out our operation. I was happy a few years later when I was informed that he had ceased to work with that gallerist. Who, it goes without saying, was evil-eyed woman No.3.

Working as an exhibition attendant at the Biennale is not really tiring, as it does not involve a lot of physical effort. But sometimes it can be very stressing because of the working conditions. In my case it feels like being jailed for six months per year, eight hours per day, six days a week, often without a proper chair to rest, no air conditioning, no lunch break, no possibility to call in sick, delaying the use of the restroom for hours, working two or even three weeks in a row with no day off when the Biennale is extraordinarily open on Mondays, in lighting conditions that some years offer only the two extremes of blinding white and sepulchral darkness, babysitting useless interns, driven mad by sounds and noises that do not differ much from those of a steel factory, mortified by the idiotic questions and nonsensical complaints of an army of visitors that soon after the beginning of every Biennale I inexorably start despising. And on top of this ordeal there is always some unexpected task to fulfill or a bizarre request to accommodate. One year a curator decided out of the blue to throw a party and asked me to find 5,200 cans of beer in a couple of days, a quantity that is not so easy to locate and buy in Venice, not to mention the delivery that can not be arranged in such a short time. So, during the hectic days of the vernissage, I had to contact a wholesaler that in turn had to contact a couple of breweries in Northern Italy to check if they had in stock such amount. A frenzied exchange of emails and phone calls ensued, in which brands, capacities, prices, discounts, and delivery options were discussed and compared. Eventually I managed to comply with the request of the curator, but he had to content himself with 2,400 cans. Sometimes it is one of the many assistants to the curator or the artist who does all he or she can do to make my life harder. For instance by rising the level of entropy of the logistical operations, making me waste time and energy to carry out pointless tasks. Once I was asked to contact a local company to ask how much it would cost to repaint the walls inside the pavilion. I inquired about the costs of the material, of the equipment they might have had to rent, of their personnel's transport and working hours, of the disposal of rubbish and special waste. I also wanted to make sure that the invoice would include the cost of VAT and that the total amount would be comprehensive of all the possible unforeseeable small jobs. While I was doing this, one of the managers of the company informed me that they had been contacted by someone working for the curator who inquired about how much they would ask to do exactly the same things, but off the book. At that point I was exonerated from my assignment, which was a relief. I do not know how the communication between the curator's assistant and the company went on, but I know that eventually the latter repainted the pavilion's walls and helped setting up the exhibition.

It is all about money: how much of it one can save, earn, or steal. Moreover, Venice is a city where the very concept of tariff is sometimes bathed in mystery. There are contractors who could offer the same service to two pavilions at two different prices. I have always suspected that shipping companies apply random charges without any fixed parameter. So, between 2018 and 2019 I carried out an experiment. I contacted some local shipping companies to check how much it would cost to transport ten crates containing artworks from either Tronchetto (the commercial port of Venice) or Mestre to an unspecified pavilion located in the Giardini. I contacted all of them twice, the first time pretending to be a foreign girl and the second one stating my real identity. In either case the quantity of crates and their dimensions and weights were the same. I compared eight carriers, and as my sex mutated from female to male they altered the value of their services. One went from 1,350 euros up to 2,200 euros, one from 1,464 euros up to 1,952 euros, the latter being the same price that was offered to my masculine self by a company that had asked 1,708 euros to my feminine side. One lowered the cost from 1,342 euros to 1,037 euros. Two other companies first asked 1,000 euros and 878 euros respectively, but when I put off my miniskirt to wear my trousers they doubled the options: I could have the crates delivered either on the bank of the canal that cuts through the Giardini or directly inside the pavilion. For one company the price shifted from 717.36 euros to 1,861.72 euros, for another one from 351.36 euros to 1,007.72 euros. Of the two remaining firms one stuck to 1,500 euros and the other one to 1,220 euros: I managed to find a tiny speck of order hidden in the chaos of Venetian transports.

Money matters at the Biennale. That is certainly not a shocking surprise. The whole city is about commerce and commodification: of souvenirs, food, accommodations, its own history and architecture. There is no reason why the Giardini and the Arsenale should be an exception. In truth, people always want more of it. More exhibitions, more venues, more parties, more jobs, more of anything that can offer fun and, especially, bring in money. That is why in the course of time locations for exhibitions have popped up like mushrooms all over Venice. They host the so-called collateral events, some of which are part of the official program of the exhibition while others are the shows that do not pass the selection process conducted by the Biennale's director or, in some cases, are run by an institution or a person that can not afford or does not bother to erode part of their budget in order to be entitled to use the official logo and be marked on the venues map distributed to whom purchases a ticket. Independent galleries host national pavilions, tiny shops turn into cozy locations for personal shows, palaces facing a languid canal or a busy street such as Strada Nuova become temporary museums for packed collective exhibitions. Even the most humid storage rooms on the ground floor of derelict buildings on the least trafficked alleys can bring a little money into their owners' wallets. A few buckets of whitewash and a sad desk at the entrance are all it takes to turn an abandoned shop or *magazzino* ('stockroom') into an exhibiting space. Indeed, there are people making a lot of money by subletting locations to rich untalented artists or to the nations that arrived too late to grab a seat at the main table of the Biennale. Obviously they provide all the support that their clients may need, from the underpaid exhibition attendants to the communication campaign (the blueprint is the same as that of the Giardini and the Arsenale: the more services one can offer, the more money they can make). The most clever of such location scouts have become successful entrepreneurs and sometimes they even curate the shows. Apart from art production they can take control of everything. Part Larry Gagosian, part Leonard Zelig, they can liaise with anyone and find a place for anything. With their Midas touch they can turn any shithole into an art venue and multiply the number of entARTainment options available to the mass of tourists who are often not even aware of the existence of the Giardini and the Arsenale. It must be said that the whole city of Venice benefits a lot from the Biennale. All the *sestieri* are livened up by the banners and the windows of the collateral events. Buildings that are usually inaccessible are opened to the public and come back to life when their centuries-old interiors host an artwork that is in sharp contrast to their decor. *Calli* and *campi* seem to take on a new identity, to have a slight chance to withstand the spread of hotels and souvenir shops. Museums and private galleries try to take part in the game (including Fondazione Prada, which is only open during the Biennale, the most prestigious catwalk of contemporary art). So, the Biennale becomes "a catalyst for different types of creative input in the city (…) a form of urbanism (…). Often the biennial is a trigger for a dynamic energy field that radiates throughout a city. This works particularly well when all the exhibition spaces and institutions in a city participate in a joint effort to form a critical mass. Biennials and other large-scale exhibitions can also trigger many self-organized side events in a city. One great potential for a biennial is that very often it becomes a spark or catalyst for something else in the local scene"[14]. However, the vast majority of those who rent their galleries and shops to independent artists and almost all the entrepreneurs who find and manage the locations of the official or unofficial collateral events could not care less about supporting Venice's art scene. What they are really after is money and provided that an individual, a cultural institution, or a ministry has some funds to spend they can accommodate any request. It is thanks to them if any self-governing patch of land on this planet can have its national pavilion at the Biennale. Thus, in 2017 the eyes of the people strolling along Strada Nuova were met by the posters advertising an exhibition hosted in one of the biggest palaces facing that same street, not far away from Ca' D'Oro. Certainly the attention of many tourists and locals was caught by a puzzling name on those posters: Kiribati. At first it might have sounded like the name of a fearless Indian coolie straight out of one of Rudyard Kipling's adventure novels. However, thanks to their smartphones they were able to find out that Kiribati is in fact the name of a place in the middle of the Pacific Ocean. It is a group of islands with little more than 100,000 inhabitants and since 1979 it is an independent country: the Republic of Kiribati. The posters on the walls and the trash cans of Strada Nuova were pointing at its official national pavilion. Which was just befitting the city context. Indeed, could an exhibition on the endangered culture of a nation made of small islands and very likely to be submerged by sea water in the next century or so not have its own spot at the Biennale of Venice, a city equally endangered by the rising sea level and itself a cluster of islets with a low number of residents and a waning identity?

In the same year San Marino's pavilion had four different locations to host a dozen artists. Given that the city state stuck in the middle of Italy counts approximately 33,000 citizens, it means that it rented a venue for every 8,250 of them. Proportionately, in the same year Germany alone should have rented around 10,000 locations to grant its 82,200,000 denizens an equal ratio of exhibiting spaces.

Either San Marino's artistic production was thousands of times higher than that of good old Deutschland or, one might venture to say, that almost invisible dot on the map of Italy was to be taken as a clear proof that nowadays the Biennale (and the western cultural field in general) has less to do with artistic research than with an all you can eat attitude that does not make any distinction between good and bad, genuine and pretentious, what belongs in museums and what should be sold at Ikea, what in fifty years time will still be topical and what is little more than fancy bric-a-brac. What matters is how much is put on display for the consumption of an inattentive public, all other criteria being regarded as hindrances to a thriving business. On their part artists will never fail to provide more than enough works. Actually, some go as far as taking part in the official collective exhibitions of countries that very probably they have never seen in their life. No need to say that this happens especially in the grey region of the collateral events. In 2015, for instance, the pavilion of Bangladesh featured also an Italian sculptor and a South African painter, whilst Kenya's one lost the patronage of the Ministry of Sports, Culture and the Arts because of the outrage that erupted when it was revealed that six out of its eight artists were Chinese (also one of the two co-curators, Ding Xuefeng, was Chinese). A couple of years before the ratio had been nine to three in favour of the non-Kenyan artists. That time, too, all the intruders except one (the Italo-Brazilian César Meneghetti) held a Chinese passport. But it is also worth noting that on both occasions the commissioner was an Italian woman named Paola Poponi and a member of the curatorial team was an Italian architect, Sandro Orlandi Stagl. In addition to that, one of the African participants was actually an Italian expatriate more successful as a hotelier in Malindi than as an artist. His name was Armando Tanzini and in 2003 he had already made an appearance on the stage of the Biennale on behalf of the Kenyan population. As said above, in 2015 the widespread indignation roused by the colonization of the Kenyan pavilion prompted minister Hassan Wario Arero to disown it and the Italian trio eventually lost the chance to see their names on the official roster of the 56th edition of the art Biennale. Since the cause of the general outrage leading to that catastrophic finale was the nationality of the people involved in the story, it is just ironic to note that the exhibition - which nonetheless was held at Isola di San Servolo, right in front of the Giardini - was titled "Creating Identities".

The Kenyan affair was not the only scandal that plagued the festival in 2015. The national pavilion of Costa Rica managed to fare even worse. Not only were the genuinely Costa Rican artists an ethnic minority in their own show, but the curator, the Italian art historian Gregorio Rossi, charged every participant 5,000 euros per work (in order, he declared, to cover the rent of the location, a palace on Riva degli Schiavoni). As often happens, the dramatis personae of the exhibition comprised a couple of catchy names. In that case they were that of an octogenarian man of letters of worldwide renown, the Nobel laureate Dario Fo, and that of an untalented starlet of yesteryear, Romina Power (daughter of the actor Tyrone Power and famous in Italy for having formed a longstanding, corny singing duo with her ex-husband). Yet one of the artists, the Italian

Umberto Mariani, managed to resist the charm of the couple of sirens hired to seduce him and his companions into renting a few square meters to display their works. He denounced the conduct of the curator and the whole story made the news. As a result the pavilion of Costa Rica was disowned, too, and became one of the many stateless collective expositions floating around the Biennale like life buoys for hopeless artists.

Many are the stories of despairing or ambitious men and women who run cash in hand to curators and critics begging to be allotted a corner in a well-lighted room and a full page entry in a cheap catalogue. It happens all the time, not just in Venice. Crooked gallerists rent their spaces to young artists promising them a breakthrough for their career. Historians ask money in exchange for a skimpy introduction to a poorly printed monograph. Magazines publish ecstatic reviews only after one has bought an advertising page. Often they work together, each one getting their share of profit. Some are so cunning and greedy that they come up with the most abject strategies to maximize their income. In 2012 during my break from the Biennale I had the misfortune to work for a small gallery run by a mediocre sculptor. Actually, the only purpose of that gallery was to exhibit his sculptures because he could not find any serious gallerist willing to represent him. Yet, he was - and very likely still is - sure of being one of the greatest living sculptors. He deluded himself to such an extent that "the sole preoccupation of his life has been himself. His ambition is to become the hero of a novel. He's spent so much time trying to convince others that he's not of this world and that fate has some mysterious trials in store for him, that he practically believes it himself"[15]. One of the consequences of his almost pathological self-worth was that he despised anybody else, including other artists. While working for him I witnessed many embarrassing scenes, heard a lot of disrespectful comments (some about me), found myself involved in uncomfortable situations and met a number of persons I did not like at first sight. I have an especially vivid recollection of something that I saw at an art fair in Beijing. We were there as guests of an Austrian gallery owned and managed by a skinny Filipino woman who kept on saying that she was about to close a deal to sell a Caravaggio and make millions of euros. In fact, I was supposed to learn from her how to sell artworks, but the only thing she seemed able to do whenever a visitor approached one of the items in her booth was to whisper in their ear "It's beautiful. Buy it!". However, something considerably more shocking than her pitiful selling technique impressed itself on my memory as an unforgettable evidence of how much some gallerists and curators care for their artists. She had subdivided the opening hours of the three-day event into two slots: morning and afternoon. Before leaving for China she had rented the walls of her booth to her artists on a time basis. They could rent a portion of space for the whole duration of the fair, for one entire day, or just for four hours. Not having been informed of her booth's time-share policy, I was dumbfounded when on the first day at around 2pm I saw her remove some paintings from the walls and substitute them with others by a different artist. Back then, it was 2012, her unexpected operation caught me off guard. But by 2015 I had witnessed and listened to so many similar stories that what happened in the Costa Rican pavilion left me quite unperturbed. Sculptors, photographers, painters and the like will always be ready to pay to exhibit at or around the Biennale and they will always find someone willing to take their money.

The art scene in Venice is quite depressing. Apart from some not too bad shows hosted by the big public museums and private galleries, most of the attempts to run a small space are doomed to frustration and economic depression. The majority of the tourists can not afford to buy art and those who can prefer to invest in Prada shoes or Louis Vuitton bags. Among the privately owned galleries, few are those that manage to support themselves by selling their goods to art collectors (more often than not they represent a very limited number of artists whose works' function is to decorate the living rooms of their buyers). Much of the local art market consists in renting locations for the Biennale. Today's art tycoons are more on a par with an estate agent than with Leo Castelli. Indeed some of them started as location scouts and eventually began to act as middlemen in order to provide all the services and personnel that might be needed (shipment, catering, press office, light technicians, decorators, exhibition attendants, etc.). Again, the more mandates the more commissions. Some content themselves with one or two spaces, others want to expand their business year by year. Some are born and raised in town, others are foreigners. Some pay taxes in Italy, others prefer to register their companies in European countries such as the Netherlands where they can benefit from low taxation rates. Some keep a low profile, others want to be larger than life and release interviews to the local dailies posing as the masterminds of the Biennale. Obviously some are honest entrepreneurs, while others hide a few skeletons in their closet. In 1995, when I was a student and had my first experience at the Biennale, I was hired by one of the latter kind. Every Sunday I had to substitute an exhibition attendant who had a second job as a waitress. The show was not far from Piazza San Marco and it was a small group exhibition representing a tiny Asian country. I worked off the books for a few weeks, but that was just a venial sin. Once I had to carry a suspiciously heavy suitcase belonging to my boss' wife to a water taxi *imbarcadero* ('landing'). Definitely not what I was supposed to be doing and no tip came to thank me for the extra service. Yet, a bit of slavery has never killed anybody. So, I put up with that too. What after so many years I still consider to be the most unprincipled thing that I had to do there, far beyond mere unprofessionalism and a telltale sign of the utmost greed, was a rather common task: selling the catalogues. Two books were printed as official publications of the exhibition. One was the real and proper catalogue of the show and the other a sort of illustrated presentation of the fine art museum that commissioned it. Both had been made with thick paper and luscious inks, their colours so bright and rich that one could not resist the temptation to touch the pictures. After all they were not very expensive, one costing 50,000 liras and the other 25,000 liras (respectively around 25 euros and 12.50 euros). Nothing was really out of this world. Except one detail: I was supposed to give the books away for free. In fact, the museum that sponsored the pavilion had intended them to be gifts for journalists, collectors, gallerists, or deeply interested visitors. But eventually my boss, aware that the two continents between himself and the museum's board of trustees guaranteed him a sure impunity, had the publications sold and every week or so he popped in to collect the proceeds. As soon as the girl I was substituting informed me about this I took extreme measures. I could not tolerate such disloyalty to take place with my complicity, letting that man who was exploiting me stuff his pockets with money that was not meant to be his. Young and leftist as I was, I thought that the only thing that I could do to restore social justice was to dust off the old Marxian doctrine and therefore I waged a campaign to redistribute the fruits of our petty crime. Since I was a not well-off student, I believed I qualified as a suitable recipient of my redistribution of income, so I started putting some banknotes in my wallet, too. I did not gain much in terms of money, but at least for the first time in my life I had the chance to face an edifying stark reality: of all the people involved in the Biennale those interested in art for art's sake are much fewer than one might imagine.

My ex boss is still around and he is certainly making a lot of money. He is not the only one. A few people succeed in becoming big players in the monopoly game of the Biennale. As already said, part of them are unquestionable professionals, while the conduct of others is a little more objectionable. Obviously money is the main thing they are after, but they never say no to anything that can come with the power they embody. Since the majority of them are males, they primarily enjoy being surrounded by young, pretty girls. They employ them in their office or to guard the exhibitions. Usually they also hire a few boys but they do not want them too close to themselves and they carefully choose those that never pose a threat to their status of alpha males. One of them, now reportedly operating mainly from the Netherlands, has a reputation for being a small-time Harvey Weinstein. I have listened to various accounts of how probing his hands can be while his female employees walk up the stairs or are focused on their job. He must also nurture the ambition to offer one more service and become a pimp, since he has been reported to ask young girls to act as escorts and go out to dinner with old, lecherous artists. I have also heard the story of a girl who was molested by him and received a sum of money under the table not to press charges against him. The most recent report of his misdeeds that was offered to me depicts a scene of arrogance and disrespect, even more detestable because it was put on at the expense of an unemployed girl who answered a vacancy ad from the internet (probably just a sham to attract new preys). She was summoned for an interview in one of the various exhibition venues he manages. Once there, she was told that he would meet her in his private apartment, not far away from that place. So she went there and another young girl led her into a room furnished with a big couch. And there he was, on that piece of furniture heir to the divans favoured by the emperors of ancient Rome to appease their carnal appetites. He was not just sitting on it. He was sprawling on it like only a person without any consideration for whoever stands in front of them can do. Like someone who can offer a job (or just pretend to do it), but only if they can take advantage of the condition of helplessness of those who look for an employment in a country overcrowded with skilled graduates that all too often have to choose between unemployment and dispiriting, dead-end occupations more fit for a trained monkey than for a human being. For him being in the position to offer an odd job to a young woman meant to have power over her, and that in turn meant that he could treat her without showing any respect and decency. Otherwise how could one explain his demeanour? The arrogance oozing into the room from his needlessly unbuttoned shirt? His hand tucked into his trousers, massaging his crotch right in front of a perfect stranger? And then his attack, in case the message was not clear enough. With a swift twist of subject he made the interview shift from the expected questions to enquiries into the girl's private life. Was she married? Engaged? Did she live with her partner? Was he an Italian or a foreigner? Was she happy? All along his investigation he fondled his ego bulging inside his trousers. Perhaps his fingers were checking if his head of human resources was aroused by the girl's skills and qualifications. No need to say that he never gave the girl the job she needed since she did not give him the job he expected.

Chapter 3: The greatest show on earth

Venice and tourists. A love-hate affair that has worsened in the last decades. It is always difficult to decide which side one has to take. Before the euro, when the lira was worth half an American dollar or about one third of a British pound, the wallets and purses of foreigners were little gold mines. When the old Italian currency's value was far lower than that of many others and only the upper classes could afford a plane ticket, a few *foresti* used to bring to town so much money that one could become rich just with the tips he got working as a hotel concierge or as a barman (back then such positions were mainly held by males and the situation has not improved much afterwards). Then everything changed: low cost flights made Venice accessible to anyone, even to people with not so much money to spend. Consequently tips decreased, tourists began looking for food in supermarkets instead of restaurants, taxi boats started offering collective rides, souvenir shops filled in their windows with trashy masks and Murano glass made in China. Today the city collapses under the weight of more than 20 million tourists (a figure calculated before the Covid-19 pandemic) that every year want to see it before it is destroyed by themselves and a citizenry unable and unwilling to restore it to its former glory. People from all over the world wander *calli* and *campielli* ('yards') unaware that what they are visiting is a dying city, a place whose canals might remind them of Amsterdam but that within a few decades might be more similar to Angkor Wat: a dead place for tourists, its urban dimension atrophied by an asphyxiating jungle of tourist-oriented facilities and businesses. They watch the cheap souvenirs on sale behind shops' windows unsuspecting that those fake traditional artifacts tell more about contemporary Venice than any story about the city that they read in the travel magazine they found on their seat on the plane to Italy. Few realize that "window displays are an immediate reflection, a quickfire snapshot of a city's personality, and not just of its outward traits, but its deepest character"[1]. On their part, most managers of restaurants are happy to ride the wave of mass tourism and to serve food and wine that are an insult to the reputation of Italian cuisine while shops selling goods that can be of any use to Venetians decrease in number and are replaced by shops of plastic bric-a-brac and souvenirs of obscure origin. Newspapers and magazines are gradually disappearing from the majority of newsstands to make room for masks and fridge magnets. Bags of multicoloured industrial pasta have invaded fruit stalls. Men's shirts with fifty buttons and three collars are offered as specimens of haute couture. It is a triumph of crass commercialism and bad taste. So, what is at stake - if not already lost - is not just the quality of what is being sold and bought, but also the aesthetic value that is attributed to Venice itself, a city that is a museum en plein air but is gradually being devoided of its elegance in order to turn it into a profitable attraction. Whoever runs a shop in Rialto, a restaurant along Strada Nuova, even a tiny bar in Via Garibaldi should bear in mind that "the city is a public space, a great exhibition space, a museum, an open book offering all kinds of subtle readings, and anyone who has a shop, a window display or any showcase of this kind has to assume a moral responsibility which requires that they stop ignoring the fact that 'their' window display might help to shape the taste of city-dwellers, help to shape the face of the city and reveal something of its essence"[2]. Yet, the city (with its history and uniqueness) is less a place to preserve than a 3D scenography to be used as a backdrop for the tourist industry. Should it be described with an allegory, one might say that Venice has become an old prostitute who gives herself to anybody that throws her some money. In order to regain her beauty before it is too late she should get rid of her pimps - those who only love her for the money they can squeeze out of her - and start offering herself to the people who show some affection and care for her instead of those who just want to have fun with her for a few hours or days. Yet, Venice is not a woman and so it can not take any decision about its own future but must suffer the consequences of the decisions taken by real human beings, in particular by the political establishment and the lobbies of the tourist industry.

Hoards of foreigners visit Venice for a few nights. Many of them are happy with saying that they have been there although they have not really seen nor grasped anything of the Serenissima. During my sleepless nights wasted working in hotels I met couples which arrived late at night, took a stroll, went to bed, and left the following morning.

A coach driver told me that a few times he had to bring groups of Chinese tourists to Florence in the morning and to Venice in the afternoon of the same day. Once in town, they would walk around the area of the bus station of Piazzale Roma and then hop back on the coach. Probably many of them left the city without knowing of the existence of Rialto and Piazza San Marco. On the other hand, quite a number of those who venture into the heart of the city do not show much respect for it. They bathe in the canals, camp in the cemetery on the island of San Michele, at night they place their sleeping bags on the waterbuses' boarding platforms or right in the middle of a *calle*. Some take the first street corner at hand as a public urinal, others have sex under the eyes of bystanders. On the *vaporetto* they keep on changing seats and annoy locals to have a better view of the palaces along Canal Grande. They climb and damage monuments, jam bridges to take a selfie, leave rubbish on windowsills and thresholds, slow down the queue at the checkouts of supermarkets to buy a can of soda, enter churches wearing clothes that would barely be enough in a swimming pool, hold and attend outdoor photography workshops with seminaked models in broad daylight. For its part, Venice lowered its overall quality to meet the demands of such tourists and to adjust to their spending power. Now it offers cheap food, cheap accommodations, cheap souvenirs, cheap culture, cheap entertainment. As long as one is not too squeamish, he or she can enjoy a speedy vacation in exchange for a few euros. Someone living in a town with many citizens or few tourists might think that such acts of commercialization are not a big deal because they happen anywhere. But in a small city like Venice they can drive someone crazy. They can lead someone to despise the very city that they used to love so much, to hate the idea of walking in the streets, entering the bars, using the public transport system, shopping. As soon as they leave their homes, residents bump into slow flocks of zombielike foreigners who do not care if the locals are late for work or rushing to the post office to pay their bills. All their daily chores are hampered while they try to wade the alien humanity flooding the streets of the city. Every day they have to cope with such situation and they can not see any viable way out of it. Regularly a bunch of motivated individuals and citizens' committees organize sit-ins and protest parades, but the impression is that the majority of residents and their elected representatives do not seem to be keen on taking any measure other than complaining about mass tourism. Every now and then the municipality imposes new hefty fines for vandalism and lewd behaviour, but that looks more like a political stunt rather than like a good way to restore order in the city. The general attitude towards the issue is of collective resignation. When they see the waterbus of line No.1 approaching the *imbarcadero* of San Toma' and they realize in horror that it is packed with tourists, Venetians roll their eyes with annoyance, aware that if God exists He is busy somewhere else. It is unlikely that they notice the stone plaque on the façade of the palace across the canal which reminds them that Lord Byron lived there at the beginning of the 19th Century. It is even less likely that they know how similar they are to their ancestors as they were depicted by the English poet. In 1818 he described them as unable to put up an appropriate protest against their city's decline. In his "Ode on Venice" he lamented that "If I, a norhern wanderer, weep for thee, | What should thy sons do? - anything but weep: | And yet they only murmur in their sleep"[3].

Like their forebears of not so long ago who had to suffer first the French and then the Austrian yoke, today's Venetians must endure the invasion of foreigners that take possession of and very often vandalize their city. They feel victimized by a rabble of *foresti* and *campagnoli* ('yokels') that infest their hometown like a plague. So much so that they do not bother any longer to draw a distinction between those who respect the city and those whose behaviour is truly barbaric. How ironic it is that the ancient Greeks and Romans, forefathers of the Italian civilization, termed 'barbarians' all foreigners, good and bad alike. And much more sadly ironic is the fact that a city that was founded on a marshland - or a swamp, to put it more crudely - in order to take refuge from the lootings of the barbarians nowadays can only survive if it lets itself be swarmed by hordes of foreigners. In fact, in spite of the nuisance they are, they carry with them the money that the city so desperately needs. It was a stinking rich Gaul who invested his money to restore and open to the public Palazzo Grassi and Punta della Dogana, the combo of exhibition venues that breathed new life into the city's art scene and soon became a recognised institution. Perhaps Monsieur François Pinault did not realize that one of the first shows that he funded, titled "Rome and the Barbarians, the Birth of a New World" (2008), could have been taken as a metaphor of the troubled yet vital relations that Venice has with its tourists. Perhaps he did not think to draw a parallel between the ancient Roman empire which was so dependent on the taxes paid by its colonies, that is to say foreign wealth, and the actual situation of Venice, a city which can only sustain itself with money coming from abroad. Probably the French magnate neither grasped the unintended symbolic meaning of "Boy with Frog", the statue by Charles Ray that he positioned in front of Punta della Dogana from 2009 to 2013. Placed on the sharp tip of Dorsoduro that sticks like a spear into the Bacino di San Marco, where Canale della Giudecca joins Canal Grande and Piazza San Marco and the island of San Giorgio Maggiore face each other, the artifact was a white statue of a big sized boy holding a frog between his fingers. Forever still, he would never let the poor amphibian plunge into the water it needed to survive. The frog, a delicate living being dependent upon the boy's whims for its own existence, bore a striking similarity to Venice itself. Not only because both could not possibly be what they were without the aquatic element. But mainly because the future of both of them was in the hands of other creatures which did not share much with them and were probably unable to comprehend their fragility. Thus a gigantic kid made of fibreglass and steel became the totemic representation of the millions of rich and poor foreigners that can make a difference in the life and death of Venice. Eventually the statue was removed. The city is still there.

Most of the visitors of the Biennale are common tourists. This may sound quite obvious, but it means that along with those who attend the various exhibitions because they are interested in contemporary art or architecture there are many who do not even know why they bought the ticket.

Many times I spoke with people who did not know if what they were visiting was the Art or the Architecture Biennale or with people who did not know about the existence of the Arsenale. One cold day in December on a waterbus that had just departed from the Lido I heard a couple ask the personnel onboard where they could buy a ticket to see the Biennale just to find out that the exhibition had closed almost one month before their trip to Venice. And in the summer of 2019 a girl asked me where the Dutch pavilion was because she wanted to visit Mark Manders' exhibition, which had ended on November 24, 2013. Then there are those who assume that the pavilions are demolished after every Biennale and the following year are rebuilt anew before the next edition. Or those who think that the artworks are thrown away at the end of the show and so ask if they can salvage them and take them home. Very often tourists want to attend the Biennale because they know that it is one of the city's most important events. Only the International Film Festival and the Redentore's fireworks can compete with it when it comes to media coverage and photo ops. When tourists ask at their hotel's front desk what to see in town, the odds are that they will be advised to visit the Biennale or the Peggy Guggenheim Collection. Both of them never let anybody down, especially if they have a very limited knowledge of contemporary art. The Guggenheim Collection comprises so many excellent works by renown masters of modern art that just reading the captions on the walls suffices to make one leave the gallery feeling a little bit more cultured. On the other hand the Biennale is so big and varied that anybody can find something for their liking. Even those who would prefer to spend the day on the beach at the Lido or browsing the souvenir shops can not but be impressed by the architectural singularities of the pavilions of the Giardini or the imposing quietness of the Gaggiandre in the Arsenale. Nobody can say no to the fun offered by the knee-deep floor of confetti of Kersten Geers and David Van Severen or by the moving trees of Céleste Boursier-Mougenot. Nor is it possible not to gape at the capsized rumbling tank of Allora & Calzadilla, at the airplane turned inside out by Roman Stańczak, at the huge squatting boy of Ron Mueck, or at the pink installation of keys of Chiharu Shiota. Sheila Hicks' big colourful skeins of wool plunge children of all ages into the magic of a classic Disney cartoon and also Ai Weiwei's flying stools seem to come from the imagination of Lewis Carroll. Meanwhile Gelitin are sticking bananas up their ass to increase the shock value of the show, pretending not to know that "complacent acceptance of the status quo may also coexist with purely spectacular rebelliousness - dissatisfaction itself becomes a commodity as soon as the economy of abundance develops the capacity to process that particular raw material"[4]. All around there are neon lights, sculptures of titanic proportions, video installations straight out of Times Square, giant hands coming out of the water, weird sounds and music, labyrinths, life-size reproductions of every human environment, paintings bigger than one's living room, blindingly white rooms that seem to have no dimensions, dark anechoic chambers, fountains, a cormanesque fog descending from the roof of the Central pavilion, coins raining from the upper floor, cars, boats, trailers, live dobermans, stuffed pigeons, a spinning cow, and plastic turtles. Then there are queues to get in, and if there is a queue it must be good. William E. Jones is even screening a vintage softcore movie in the Central pavilion. No matter if there is a corpse floating in the swimming pool before the entrance of Elmgreen & Dragset's Nordic pavilion or if a look at Roberto Cuoghi's gang of dying Christs is a trip to Auschwitz. And who cares if Christoph Büchel exhibits a boat in which hundreds of migrants died as if it were a prop from a disaster movie - the most accomplished exercise in bad taste offered by the art world in the last decades. It is all part of the fun and Carsten Höller's carousel is there precisely to remind each and everyone that the Biennale is a fairground in disguise. It is a theme park, like Venice itself. Indeed many of its visitors, perhaps the majority, expect to be amused and if they are not they think there must be something wrong with it. They approach the Biennale with the same mindset they have when they watch a reality show on television, therefore they demand that what they are offered is a kind of light entertainment which their brains can take in as one more tv programme. After all, it is television that "has made entertainment itself the natural format for the representation of all experience. Our television set keeps us in constant communion with the world, but it does so with a face whose smiling countenance is unalterable. The problem is not that television presents us with entertaining subject matter but that all subject matter is presented as entertaining, which is another issue altogether. To say it still another way: entertainment is the supra-ideology of all discourse on television. No matter what is depicted or from what point of view, the overarching presumption is that it is there for our amusement and pleasure"[5]. And since "television is our culture's principal mode of knowing about itself (...) how television stages the world becomes the model for how the world is properly to be staged. It is not merely that on the television screen entertainment is the metaphor for all discourse. It is that off the screen the same metaphor prevails"[6]. One might object that nowadays the internet and social networks have replaced television, but what are Netflix, Facebook, Instagram, Twitter and finally computers themselves if not the technological evolutions of the good old tv set? Therefore, what many of Biennale's visitors look for is pure entARTainment, an all you can eat art event where they can gorge themselves without giving a second thought to what they are absorbing. And they can really be served anything. Once an art critic that did not like the exhibition I was guarding asked me "What does this tell us that we don't know already?". He wanted to say that there was nothing fresh in that show, that it was basically a useless display of artistic commonplaces. I did not know what to say and so I did not attempt to reply, but some years later I know what I should have said: that for many visitors of the Biennale anything is new, never seen before, unprecedented. That does not necessarily mean that they find everything stimulating, but rather that they are keen on labelling as contemporary art anything that they are sold as such without being able to draw a line between what is good and what is bad, what is original and what is not, what is ahead of its time and what belongs in the past, what in the future will be regarded as an accomplished bitter commentary on the early 21st Century and what will be forgotten like any disposable piece of cheap furniture. So, they can be fed anything and keep on doing just what they are supposed to do: take part in the game in order to help beat the previous year's attendance record.

It is impossible to describe the average visitor of the Biennale. All ages, cultures, religions, ethnicities, social classes, levels of education, sexual orientations are represented, although their combination may vary from year to year. Needless to say, Italians make up the most numerous nationality. But all foreigners combined amount to at least half of the attendants. It would take a real leap of faith just to take into consideration the idea that they are all art or architecture lovers. In fact, they could be subdivided into three main categories: people really interested in art and architecture who try to expand their knowledge or simply to catch up with what is going on; people who like to picture in their minds an image of themselves projected into the art world; the already mentioned people who would find it difficult to explain why they are there. Italian teachers and students are a couple of typologies that span all the three categories. They are supposed to be inscribed in the first one and in fact some of them are, but the biggest portion belongs in the other two, with an astonishing inclination towards the third one. Pupils of primary schools are too young to understand what is happening around them. They must be excused if they are only attracted by what is colourful and looks fun. Teenagers are expected to be more conscious of what surrounds them and to grab the opportunity to learn something new without having to bend their backs on their textbooks. That is very seldom the case. More often than not they take their excursion to the Biennale for a day off school, a vacation during which they put their brains in stand-by mode and hang about with their pals. And so do almost all of their teachers. Usually as soon as they pass the turnstiles at the entrance they gather their classes and give them the instructions they have been waiting to utter throughout their drowsy trip to Venice by coach or train. I have heard them uncountable times. It is a refrain that testifies to how little too many teachers care for the education they are giving to their students. More or less their instructions go as follows: "Now go wherever you want to go and do whatever you want to do. Just make sure that at 5pm you are all near the exit so we can catch the waterbus and go back home". And off they go, students and teachers alike, each their own way and praying God not to run into each other before it is time to leave. Small groups of juvenile delinquents rove the pavilions to molest other visitors, mock the exhibition attendants, vandalize the artworks, steal any object they can lay their hands on, doodle idiocies on the visitors' books. Meanwhile other groups sit on the benches in the park and lobotomize themselves with their smartphones or eat food whose packaging ends up anywhere but in the trash bins. All along their teachers sip coffee at the restaurant and walk idly around trying to keep away from them. Certainly this is inappropriate, utterly unprofessional, even immoral on the grounds that their mission is to be a guiding light for their students during the years in which they start building up their education and personality. If so, then what can be said about the teachers that do accompany their students on their tour only to give them explanations they make up on the spot and which have absolutely nothing to do with what they have in front of them? They speak about anything except the history of art. Once I heard a teacher that in order to be plain with his students told them that he did not "give a fuck" about the installation they were looking at. Such things happen because the teaching profession has always been a fallback for many Italian graduates and unsurprisingly a lot of them look forward to their retirement day since the very first moment they step into a classroom.

If not with their teachers, teenagers and children visit the Biennale accompanied by their parents. Mum and dad are happy to introduce their offspring to the phantasmagoric world of contemporary art. They feel modern and cool, more caring than other couples which can only think about a Pixar movie if asked to choose a cultural activity for the whole family. The mere idea of making their kids pass a few hours among installations and architectural models enraptures so much most of the parents (at least 80%) that they believe they need not do anything else than buying the tickets. Usually they do not let their children loose like many remiss teachers do, but they show the same concern for their progeny's education and safety. They never try to explain anything to them, nor do they care if they disturb other people or wreak havoc on the exhibitions. Their sole purpose is to enjoy the show while their children, so they hope, soak up art concepts through their skin pores. They leave all their parental responsibilities at the cloakroom near the main entrance and do not restrain their sons and daughters from doing anything. They pretend not to see them when they stamp their greasy hands on a photograph or climb a sculpture made of wax. They look the other way when they run screaming among the few people that still think that quietness is de rigueur. Sometimes they completely forget about their children's safety. In 2014, during the successful Architecture Biennale directed by Rem Coca-Koolhaas, the Architectural Association School of Architecture of London built a wood installation in front of the Central pavilion. It was a life-size copy of Le Corbusier's Maison Dom-ino, a two storey house that was about eight metres high. Only its supporting structure was mounted. It consisted of two floors, a flat roof, six beams, and four flights of stairs. There were not walls, so one could see through the building. Since there was no parapet or anything else to prevent the visitors from falling down from the first floor or the roof, access to the house was prohibited. An employee of the Foundation was supposed to keep an eye on it from the entrance of the Central pavilion. One day, when the sun was setting and the natural light at the Giardini was dimmer, I was getting some air on the threshold of my pavilion. I looked in the direction of the Maison Dom-ino and on its top I spotted a small, undefined figure moving around like one of those leprechauns caught on cctv that kept me company from Youtube during my night shifts as hotel concierge. I realized it was a kid aged ten or so and that he was alone on the roof of the installation. He was running and jumping unnoticed by the visitors and the workers of the Biennale. Unlike an average adult he was not afraid to stand on the border of the roof. Being the only child in that big empty house and watching the world of the grown-ups from far above their heads must have made him feel like a small king. If there is one thing that all children have in common, that thing is the joy that comes from finding a place of their own, be it the attic in their home or an abandoned old building. They like experiencing the independence which is not yet granted to them. Very likely that small child on the wooden roof was busying himself with so many thoughts and fantasies that he could not possibly be bothered with an estimate of the dangers lurking in the darkness of an edifice without walls - a house that seemed to have been built with the sole purpose to let people fall down from it. The person who was supposed to make sure that nobody entered into the Maison Dom-ino was not in sight. I presumed he was inside the Central pavilion, guarding one of its rooms. That was and still is the Foundation's policy (shared by many national pavilions) towards the safety of the visitors and the protection of the artworks: always much more preferable to take some risks and save money on personnel's costs than paying employees which, if nothing goes wrong, might give the idea of being redundant. Having one person guard four rooms and keep one's fingers crossed always looks much more convenient than chipping the show's budget to prevent injuries and damages which the endemic Italian optimism forbids to take into consideration. So, the person who had also been charged with the surveillance of the replica of Le Corbusier's work was not around and could not stop that child from jeopardizing his life. But what about the kid's parents? They were nowhere to be seen. I could not see anybody near the installation that might have been his mother or father. Nor anybody else showing any sign of apprehension for his fate. Fortunately, when I was about to head for the Maison Dom-ino after having considered all this, the child grew tired of his game and went down the stairs to reach safer ground. He run away alone and disappeared from my view as swiftly as he had entered it. I assume he continued his solitary peregrinations for a little longer and, once fed up with them, he rejoined his family. Certainly he told his mum and dad about his adventure on the top of the installation and probably they congratulated him on his feat without even imagining the risks he had taken. They had let him wander alone at dusk in a big park full of strangers, a place that offered him many chances to harm himself or to damage expensive exhibits. Very likely they were not much concerned with his safety in the first place, either out of pure neglect or because of their inability to grasp the complexity of the environment they had chosen for their family excursion.

All's well that ends well, nonetheless at the Biennale parental irresponsibility manifests itself all the time. One year one of the rooms of the pavilion I was working in had a ladder leading to a dark attic. Usually that room was off limits for the visitors, being a service space where only authorized personnel were admitted. However, the curators decided to incorporate that small room in the exhibition. Everybody (including myself) assumed that it was obvious that the visitors could not possibly think that they were being asked to climb a steep ladder ending on a dark upper floor. It was agreed that nobody in their right minds would ever think of putting their feet on its rungs and consequently no "do not climb" sign was hung on the wall. That was an unclever decision. Many visitors tried to reach the attic, and surely many managed to do so when I was not there to stop them. But what really shocked me was the attitude of an Italian mother that I caught encouraging her son, not over six or seven years of age, to climb the ladder to the top and reach the attic which, as far as she could see, was a mysterious place bathed in darkness beyond a hatchway. When I arrived the child was almost halfway there. I immediately reproached his mom not only for letting but also for prompting him to risk getting hurt. In reply, she said that it was our fault because we did not write anywhere that it was prohibited to climb the ladder. As if a mother really needed an explicit signal on the wall in order to establish if her little son might fall from a ladder and get injured as it often happens even to adults. Her behaviour was the paradigm of two attitudes that are so frequent at the Biennale: parents' claim of being unaccountable for what happens to or is done by their children and a generalized conviction in being allowed to do anything that is not specifically prohibited.

Sometimes it seems like common sense has been wiped off the face of the planet. Yet, the real issue lies much deeper than that. The lack of a proper education, a violent resurgence of human stupidity triggered by social media, a widespread disrespect for the others, and a rising level of socially condoned aggressivity are the four main personality traits of an impressive number of persons who visit Venice and the Biennale. Both the city and the exhibition can be taken as case studies to measure the level of decadence of western civilization (it must be kept in mind that the majority of the tourists visiting Venice come from Europe, the USA, and other regions of the world that have been shaped by western culture). During my service at the Biennale I have seen all sorts of attitudes that up until the beginning of this century were inconceivable inside a museum or simply in public. While working there I have seen people belching, farting, screaming, shouting on their cellphone, singing, whistling, eating, drinking alcohol, quarrelling, fighting, dancing, picking their noses, poking their hands into other people's bags, cleaning their teeth with dental floss in front of the artworks, taking off their shoes to apply band aids to the blisters on their feet or removing their sandals to rub off the dirt between their toes, spitting and throwing rubbish on the floor, sleeping on the benches. I and almost all my colleagues have suffered thefts of our personal belongings, insults, threats, mockery, all sorts of bad treatment that could only be responded to with a spit in the face of their perpetrators. I have seen, heard, and smelled so many things that are so far from the finesse that is supposed to reign in the world of art and the humanities that I am now fully convinced that all is lost and it is high time to commission Arvo Pärt a requiem for western culture. But before it is too late, it might be worth trying to improve the environment of the Biennale by posting a list of basic rules on the Foundation's website, a few principles that the visitors should be invited (forced, in my dreams) to comply with. Perhaps a decalogue along the lines of the following one: "1) In case you have the intention of cracking a joke or saying something smart, take into consideration that very probably the exhibition attendant has to listen to that very same thing at least ten times every single day. So, do not expect he or she to be amused by your story. 2) The pavilion that represents your country is not an embassy or a consulate and therefore the exhibition assistant is not supposed to speak your language or give you any assistance other than information about the show. 3) Odds are that the exhibition attendant that you treat like a retarded person has a level of education that your entire family put together could never equal. Do not delude yourself into believing that you stand on a higher moral ground just because you were more lucky in your job hunt. 4) Imposing a dress code at the Biennale might be regarded as undemocratic, but on the other hand filling in a public space with your bad taste is a form of violence exerted upon the others. So, if you go to the Biennale sporting flip-flops or have not taken a bath in the last two weeks do not be surprised if the exhibition attendants treat you like a moron. You are. 5) There is no museum or gallery in the world that will let you in five minutes before closing time. Surprising as it may seem, it is simply idiotic to bang on the door of a pavilion if you find it closed at 5.55pm. Especially if you have spent the whole day sunbathing on the grass near the Stirling pavilion instead of visiting the exhibition. 6) If you spent a lot of money to travel to Venice and to sleep and eat there try to enjoy your holiday: do not spoil it by keeping a grudge and grabbing any opportunity to quarrel with the exhibition attendants of the Biennale. 7) If you are successful in your trade that does not mean that you are knowledgeable about contemporary art. Never lose the opportunity to keep your mouth shut and abstain from trying to explain the meaning of an artwork to an exhibition assistant who spends six months near it. 8) If you are a student do not mock the exhibition attendants and think that they are all losers - I did the same when I was in my twenties. Nowadays the job market is far from being prosperous and even people with a higher education end up having to accept lousy jobs to make ends meet. In the worst case scenario you will end up doing the same thing. And for at least the next twenty years the worst case scenario is the only possible scenario. 9) If you are not happy with the rules of a pavilion (such as not taking pictures, not eating, keeping quiet, taking off your shoes, leaving your umbrellas by the entrance door, etc.) just leave without complaining. Nobody broke into your house at night and dragged you to the Biennale threatening to kill your children and dog. It was your own choice and you must visit it without expectations and preconceptions. Moreover, it is not in the exhibition attendants' power to establish rules, therefore do not take it out on them. 10) When you visit an exhibition do not be a dick. Be polite and do not be aggressive. Odds are that you do not belong there and that the exhibition attendants do not slap your face only because they do not want to lose their job. Do not mistake politeness for submissiveness or for a display of sincere respect that you clearly do not deserve". Certainly these ten commandments of politeness and common sense alone could not suffice to fully restore civility, considering that less than 5% of the visitors would obey them or even go through the trouble of reading them. But at least they might be used, along with many others, as abstract signposts showing the way towards a better bahavior on the part of the visitors.

In 2011 the main room of the exhibition I was guarding had been darkened because it hosted a visual installation consisting of seven video projections juxtaposed to each other. One day I went in that room to inspect it and spotted a black thing on the floor. Even from a distance I was immediately able to determine that it did not belong there: having swept and mopped the floor hundreds of times I knew all its imperfections and that dark shape was definitely not a mottle on one of its stone slabs. At first I thought it might be a spot of coffee spilt by one of the innumerable persons unable to have a drink or an icecream without dropping at least half of it in front of someone else who will walk on it and leave a trail of sticky footprints all over the pavilion. Then I realized that it was creased, so I thought that it might be a dry leaf. But the more I neared it the more it lost its imperfect flatness and, once before it, I found out that I had been deceived by darkness and perspective. Indeed it had a volume that expressed itself in an irregular shape, the whole thing being as big as a medium-sized meringue. My eyes could not figure out what it was exactly, but its surface appeared smooth and emanating an air of quietness and softness. While the feeble lights of the video projectors flickered around it, that object almost seemed to transcend itself. I bent over to pick it up but, on second thought, I decided that it was safer to touch it with the tip of my shoe first. My impression was right, it was soft. It was a clod of humid soil that had stuck on the bottom of someone's shoe or that had been brought in by a toddler. So I fetched my broom and dustpan to dispose of it. When I lifted it from the floor I made a new startling discovery: it stank, and it did it so foully that I withdrew my head in disgust and realized that I had been wrong when I had reached my conclusion regarding its nature. It was fecal matter. Or, to put it bluntly, shit. Someone had left a small pile of excrements right in the middle of the exhibition's main room. Presumably they had been expelled by a dog (most probably a pug, being the most hideous canine breed that has ever trampled on Earth) whose owner must have had a connection with it that was much stronger than that of a simple leash – a man or a woman whose civic spirit was as developed as that of their dog. I also pondered over the possibility that a fan of Piero Manzoni had squatted and shat on the floor to start a new form of art criticism, or that someone had carried with them a plastic bag containing their baby's poop with the aim of emptying it at the Biennale to protest against the commodification of contemporary art. Eventually I ruled out both options, since it would have taken too much time, effort, and daring to accomplish them. After all, once a dog tinkled in my pavilion. Why should another one not have taken the liberty of going solid?

Sooner or later anybody working at the Biennale loses their temper and has an argument with a visitor. It depends on how patient and how stressed one is, but usually during each edition it happens to everybody a number of times. Some visitors are edgy by nature, others are pissed off because they waste the first day of their vacation looking for their b&b and the remaining two suspecting that everybody in town is trying to rip them off. Some feel mistreated by a city that may turn out to be much less hospitable than it appears on a postcard sent by a friend and consume their nerves complaining about anything as if that were their way to seek redressal. So, they visit the Biennale with a vengeance and as soon as they have the chance they take it out on the exhibition attendants or the turnstile operators and rain all their repressed hostility upon them. Sooner or later everybody gets involved in a row started by a petty misunderstanding, but there are times when one has to deal with visitors which are deliberately impolite. For instance people wanting to enter by the exit located a few meters from the actual entrance or going behind a desk to rummage through an exhibition attendant's personal belongings. Or tour guides who keep on talking in an excessively loud voice even if they have been asked not to do so. Once a woman took possession of my laptop in my absence and went through my emails. Obviously when I saw what she was doing and urged her to stop she reacted as if it were I who was being rude. Some people truly believe that they can do anything they want and that nobody has the right to stop them. If there is one single term that can be used to describe them, that word is 'asshole'. In fact, an asshole "systematically allows himself to enjoy special advantages in interpersonal relations out of an entrenched sense of entitlement that immunizes him against the complaints of other people (…) The asshole does what he does out of a 'sense of entitlement,' a sense of what he deserves, or is due, or has a right to. However misguided, the asshole is morally motivated. He is fundamentally different from the psychopath, who either lacks or fails to engage moral concepts, and who sees people as so many objects in the world to be manipulated at will. The asshole takes himself to be justified in enjoying special advantages from cooperative relations. Given his sense of his special standing, he claims advantages that he thinks no one can reasonably deny him"[7]. That explains why there are so many people who enjoy doing things which they know that can be an annoyance for the persons working at the Biennale. They like disregarding their dignity and they want to make sure that their victims are aware of that. They treat them with the same contempt that the kings and queens of antiquity had for their servants. They are those who still think that in a restaurant they can deal with waiters and waitresses as if they were slaves in a cotton plantation of the 18th Century. Not only do they never apologize for being rude, they do not even acknowledge one's right to protest against their behaviour. Such individuals are "wholly immunized against the complaints of others. Whether or not the complaint is ultimately reasonable, the person is not registered, from the asshole's point of view, as worthy of consideration. The person who complains is not seen as a potential source of reasonable complaint but is simply walled out. If the person complaining is 'standing up for herself,' in order to be recognized, it is as though she were physically present but morally nonexistent in the asshole's view of the world (…) Assholes are especially outrageous in a crucial way: they don't even offer a show of respect. A show of respect is, after all, a form of respect, however unsatisfactory. We don't make a show of respect to a fence post, since it isn't the kind of thing to which respect is even in principle owed. With people, by contrast, showing respect is all important for good relationships, whether in international diplomacy, life in the workplace, or friendship and intimate relationships"[8].

Assholism is one of the most likely causes of quarrels, while their intensity is determined by a visitor's level of aggressiveness. Such ratio can vary a lot according to a number of personal and circumstantial factors. For instance one's temperament or how positively he or she can react to the humid, stifling August heat. Many are the variables that must be considered in order to attempt to establish an individual's level of bellicosity at any given moment. It would be necessary to carry out a multidisciplinary research (psychological, sociological, anthropological) to sketch a chart of fixed parameters to be used in conjunction with the study of every single person's biography. Probably one day Facebook's algorithms and subdermal chips will make this possible, but for the time being the only thing that the personnel of the Biennale can do is to refrain from starting an argument with a visitor. In fact, very often attempting to discuss with some visitors in order to talk sense into them is a dive into the unfathomable sea of human psychology. The exhibition attendant who tries to explain to someone why they cannot touch an artwork or the turnstile operator who tries to make someone else understand that on the back of their ticket it is clearly stated that it entitles them to only "1 entry to each of the two exhibition venues" will very likely find themselves arguing with people who simply do not know and have no intention to comply with any rule which limit their freedom to do anything they feel like doing. Such people live and act by their own logic and values, so much so that they regard as irrational and oppressive anybody and anything that might stand in their way. They are so self-centred, absorbed in their needs and whims, that they lose the ability to recognize others as human beings and so they tend to disrespect any form of authority that is not equipped with a uniform and a gun. For them the whole world is populated by mannequins that they can push and knock without having to restrain themselves or apologize. Therefore, whoever happens to interact with one of these persons must be "open to the possibility of experiencing oneself as an object of his experience and thereby of feeling one's own subjectivity drained away. One is threatened with the possibility of becoming no more than a thing in the world of the other, without any life for oneself, without any being for oneself"[9]. Being aware of this is fundamental to survive in an environment like the Biennale where one is surrounded by hundreds of assholes and literally feels as being kept prisoner by them, since he or she can not just quit and go home. Of course every now and then one gets sick and tired of being treated like an animal and flips out, suddenly remembering that "if you're a human being, then you reserve the right to complain, to protest. If you give up that right, then you cease to exist"[10], but quarrelling - which I have done many times - is very seldom the right answer. The best thing to do, as far as I am concerned, is to struggle to become impervious to impoliteness and disrespect, if possible to enter in a state of temporary autism in order to shut myself off from the bullshit I am exposed to. To dissociate my mind from my tongue, letting the former lose itself in an undetectable reverie while the latter mechanically utters complaisant words of deference that do not need to be thought over because I have already pronounced them uncountable times. And I am sure that I am not the only one to adopt this strategy of survival, which must date back to the first time two human beings met each other in the wilderness, for "it is well known that temporary states of dissociation of the self from the body occur in normal people. In general, one can say that it is a response that appears to be available to most people who find themselves enclosed within a threatening experience from which there is no physical escape. Prisoners in concentration camps tried to feel that way, for the camp offered no possible way out either spatially or at the end of a period of time. The only way out was by a psychical withdrawal 'into' one's self and 'out of' the body. This dissociation is characteristically associated with such thoughts as "This is like a dream", "This seems unreal", "I can't believe this is true", "Nothing seemed to be touching me", "I cannot take it in", "This is not happening to me", i.e. with feelings of estrangement and derealization. The body may go on acting in an outwardly normal way, but inwardly it is felt to be acting on its own, automatically"[11]. Usually I agree on any nonsense that is uttered by my interlocutors just to get rid of them as soon as possible, as Marcel Duchamp used to do whenever someone wanted to have an argument with him. Or I lie through my teeth or put the blame for my faults on someone else. For instance when people, usually old women, complain because there is no information material about the exhibition that they can bring home. I pretend that I gave away the last brochure just two minutes ago (whereas I did it three months before) and that a new delivery is due the following day (which will not happen, but sometimes I just enjoy being sadistic). Or when I need to go to the toilet but can not leave the pavilion unattended and so I close it for five minutes and then tell the people who have been waiting outside that I had to do it in order to fix a technical problem. When questioned by an inquisitive visitor I pretend that my shortcomings and mistakes, for example when I have not had time to mop the floor or have forgotten to switch on a video projection, are the faults of my nonexistent colleagues. I could say anything to avoid having too long a conversation with someone who looks like being keen to argue, moan, or complain. Sometimes I just pretend to be stupid in order to be left alone, but there are days when even I lose my temper and confront a visitor to the point of quarrelling. Indeed, some people really bring out the worst in me. For instance arrogant journalists, aggressive douchebags, adults behaving like clowns to be the centre of attention, thieves, teachers who do not restrain their students, people who make noise or litter the pavilion, anybody who is impolite or disrespects me, the artists, or the artworks, people who are simply too stupid to live or deny the obvious even when they are caught red-handed. Like those who say that they did not touch an artwork while their hands are still on it or those who try to unfasten a display catalogue to steal it and when busted say that they thought it was intended to be taken for free. I try my best to put up with all this, to keep calm and sublimate my anger into a sort of apathetic fatalism which, as frustrating as it is, at least does not get me into trouble. However, sometimes I flip out and order someone to go out immediately or tell them that I am not paid to make them happy and do not give a shit about their remarks. I never shout or threaten, I just make my point and try to make them understand that the ticket they bought does not entitle them to push me around or behave like boors. I do not know if I succeed, but my aim is to communicate that although I do not use an abusive language inside of me I just feel contempt for them, that I despise them yet prefer not to express it to maintain a minimum level of civility.

Although an exhibition attendant does not do much, it can be quite trying to work at the Biennale - especially in the summer heat, when it rains, or on the busy weekends of the last month, when it feels like working in a shopping mall during sales season. One gets tired of seeing so many people and answering the same questions over and over again. Usually my ability to cope with the rest of humanity is at its highest peak for three or four weeks after the vernissage, when I am still fresh after the winter break. Then my patience and amiability start to wane and eventually give way to intolerance. I very seldom express my feeling of annoyance but I secretly despise a good portion of visitors for their attitudes and attires. Since I can not leave my post, very often not even to eat or go to the toilet when I most need to, I feel like I am being held captive by people whose only goal in life is to annoy me and drain the place where I work of anything that can ease my agony of being there. They seem to plan things in advance. For example when foreigners interrupt me when I am reading a good book to ask me a question in their faltering Italian, insist that I reply in Italian and then ask me to repeat the same thing in English because they have not understood a single word of what I have said. Some enjoy interrupting me when I am talking on the phone or writing an email to ask a question that is not remotely related to the exhibition. Others look at me from a certain distance and wait until the very moment I put in my mouth a cracker to come to me and force me to gulp it down, dry as a spoonful of sand, in order to satisfy their dull, untimely curiosity. Nor do they let me enjoy more than a few minutes of silence. They scream, whistle, sing, fart, belch, append clanking objects to their backpacks, drag their feet, shout at other people across the pavilion, talk loudly on their cell phones. Once I heard a phone ring for quite a long time from inside the pocket of a middle aged man. When I realized that he could not hear it either because of deafness or because his head was lost in the clouds, I approached him and informed him that his phone was ringing (less to do him a favour than to hint that he was disturbing all the people around him and especially me). His reply was that he was well aware of that but he did not feel like answering the call and so he just preferred to let it go on ringing. If it is not my hearing sensibility that is offended it is my sense of smell that must suffer the fumes of garlic exhaling from the skin of Chinese women, the body odour of Frenchmen who do not shower for the whole duration of their holidays, the farts released by old people with rotting bowels just a metre away from where I am sitting, the stink of feet that revel in a pair of Birkenstock sandals like pigs in a sty, the stale smell of tobacco and nicotine trapped in dirty clothes, or the nauseating smell of cheap ham that lingers around some people until the digestion of their lousy sandwich is complete. My sense of sight does not fare much better, though the Biennale is supposed to be a place and a state of mind filled with beauty and good taste. Indeed many visitors display aesthetic sophistication and propriety, but unfortunately they are not enough to counterbalance the theatre of visual horrors put up by an ever increasing number of tasteless, graceless visitors. There are moments in which one might think that the real show is not made up by the art installations assembled in the various pavilions but rather by the people that are in front of them. So, the Giardini and the Arsenale turn into huge cabinets of free-range human curiosities that would surely be of interest to a research team of scientists and men of letters on a quest to find out how and why nowadays it is so hard to escape from a world in which objects, buildings, furniture, artworks, language, music, food, and clothes look and function in utter discordance with all the things in western culture and daily life that for so many centuries have aroused, shaped, and then appeased humankind's longing for all those qualities that can be roughly comprised within the generic concept of beauty. Certainly there are many reasons for such a state of things, yet one that comes abruptly to the fore at the Biennale is that people have (voluntarily or without realising it) become ugly and tasteless, so indifferent to the vulgarity they are exposed to that they unknowingly add to it with their demeanour and attire. I am sure she meant no harm to me or to the rest of humanity, however the German woman aged between seventy-five and eighty who stood in front of me proffering her bony ass vacuum-packed by a pair of transparent white jeans did make this planet a less agreeable place. She could not imagine that the g-string cutting through her ass like dental floss stuck halfway into a lump of expired beef jerky was not only plainly visible to anybody, but was also a sight that killed any hint of eroticism which that garment usually offers. She just wanted to keep her ass cool, but to do so she doused the sexual heat of every male that happened to walk behind her. On the other hand young girls can do worse. In 2014 I was sitting in the main room of my pavilion and was admiring young girls' bums. I have always been partial to women's asses, so I can spend minutes following them with my eyes. Waiting for a good chance to appreciate their shapes and volumes, especially when the sunlight filters through their skirts and illuminates their panties like divine revelations. That day, I was sitting on a chair when a young girl, aged twenty or so, stopped in front of me with her back to me. She was talking to some friends, a language that I could not fully grasp but thought to be Portuguese. She was dark-skinned, so I imagined she was Brazilian. Indeed she had a stunning curvy body, long black wavy hair, plump bosom, and wore a white short dress. She was standing right in front of me when the miracle happened. She bent forward and the more she did so the more her dress was lifted by her round ass. First her thighs came into view. Smooth and shiny like polished wood. Then a tiny portion of her white panties. But as her dress was lifted a bit more and finally revealed the whole of her ass, what promised to be a paradisiacal spectacle turned into a hellish vision. Hers was not a bum but a rump, so hairy that it looked like she was giving birth to an orangutan. Black hair popped out of her panties like a new form of vegetation spreading from a warm, humid crevice. It looked somewhat menacing, too, so I had to divert my eyes and scan the room for another ass. Such is life at the Biennale. Even the joy of sexual fantasies can be marred by an unfortunate twist of fate. Or it can happen that a sexual intercourse is offered by the wrong person at the wrong time. For instance when I was working in a dark pavilion which had been painted black from floor to ceiling and did not have any source of light apart from the feeble natural light coming in from the roof which had been covered with a black screen, too. One day I was standing by an emergency exit door, opening and closing it to help people out while preserving the darkness of the pavilion. At some point an old woman, aged seventy or so, approached the exit with her grandchild because they wanted to leave. But when I opened the door they wavered a bit on the threshold and therefore I shut the door again not to let in too much light. As soon as total blackness was restored around us, the old woman tried to get hold of the kid to lead him out of there. I presume she was trying to reach for his hand, but she actually grabbed my crotch and started pulling, saying "Come, come!". I immediately tried to stop her but my pleas took some seconds to travel from her old ears to her brain, which in turn employed some more time to process the information and give her hand the order to let go of what she wrongly thought was the kid's arm (no need to say that the last part of this sentence is a self-flattering guess). Thus, after a few long seconds of sexual horror I managed to get rid of that old woman and her grandchild, who could never have imagined that his granny was a molester of exhibition attendants. That said, it is only natural that the personnel of the pavilions have sex inside them before or after the opening hours. Young and attractive boys and girls work in a very promiscuous environment, often spending more time at the Biennale than at home. I can not believe that they are never aroused by the chemical reactions triggered by their bodies and brains. I am sure that there are couples - either steady ones or formed on the spot - who at 6pm go for a quickie in the storeroom or right in front of an installation. It even happened to me, who surely do not qualify as a Latin lover. Once in my twenties, with a beautiful tall girl who looked like a French top model. Then again in my late thirties, with a stocky cheap girl with saggy tits. I deduce that the attractiveness of each girl was inversely proportional to my age. It figures. I read it all in John Keats' poems when I was a young student, but I did not imagine that the quantity of beauty allotted to me would become so scarce so soon.

Obviously summer is the best (or rather the worst) season to admire people's ugliness. Not only do they wear horrible shorts and tank tops which let sweat drip from their armpits, they rejoice in sporting sandals even if their feet's toenails are infested with fungi. Looking at visitors' feet I have seen all the hues of green ranging from dark yellow to pale blue. They say that sandals with socks are gross, but in some cases it would be better to dispense with fashion rules. Things do not go much better if one's eyes go up. For some gay girls legs have become a battle ground in their war to assert their gender. Some have limbs so hirsute that it is difficult to distinguish them from those of a man. And even if one gets used to that, what about girls shaving their face to grow a moustache or even a full beard? That will never stop puzzling me. I do not think to be a sexist reactionary, yet a girl or a woman wearing a Carhartt outfit and Dr. Martens boots topped with facial hair in order to look like an employee of a gas station to me is such a waste of femininity that goes far beyond any gender expression that I can conceive of. I am aware of my cultural limitations and regret them, but such a sight is really unbearable for me. Just not to seem too misogynist, I add that I found much more disgusting that man who one day walked into my pavilion wearing a pair of short jeans whose waist was so low that his pubic hair stuck out of it like a tuft of dried grass. One more millimetre and I would have had to call the police and have him arrested for public indecency. However, even when people do not expose their most private parts, their faces suffice to fill the ambiance with ugliness. Actually, sometimes they manage to reach the highest levels of disfigurement in their pursuit of an unnatural ideal of beauty. Plastic surgery, lifting, and Botox are their means of transforming their faces into replicas of a model that nobody has ever seen. Russian women start pumping up their cheeks and lips when they are still quite young, as if an inflated face were a status symbol to display like a diamond ring. Once I saw a young mother with her child, aged five or six, who had modified her face to such an extent that her son could not possibly have any memory of her real lineaments in his mind. In a few years she accomplished what took Orlan her entire career to achieve. At least American women start when they are approaching middle age. And apparently they never stop. I have seen old American women who had lifted and stretched the skin of their faces so many times that their nipples ended up on their cheeks. An army of dying people trying to deceive the Grim Reaper by gaining a couple of years at the cost of losing their identities and dignity.

The personnel of the Biennale who have an interest in shamanism and have to deal with a visitor can try to guess what is the power animal of their interlocutor and behave accordingly. Everybody has their own and for sure the bear, the deer, the snake, the jaguar, and the other popular guardian spirits from Mexico or Siberia are all present though invisible. However, the power animals that seem to accompany most of the visitors and inspire their behaviour are birds. Not the hawk or the eagle but the very same birds that live in the Giardini: blackbirds, pigeons, seagulls. The first species is not as common as the other two and indeed they protect a kind of visitors that is on the brink of extinction. They are peaceful and friendly even though they are not really at ease because of the noisy crowd. They fly around looking for nourishment (mainly berries, the best food that the flora of the Giardini can offer them) without making noise or disturbing the other living beings. They mind their own business and hop under the shade of trees in such a quiet manner that their presence is hardly noticed. It goes without saying that they watch over the few people who still like attending an exhibition in silence, those who come and go without attracting anybody's attention. Visitors who hardly make themselves noticed and typify the ideal exhibition-goers: quiet, polite, well-informed, unbiased, sensitive, curious about what they see. The individual that immediately springs to mind when one thinks about an art lover. Unfortunately, being a positive stereotype, such individual is seldom sighted in the real world. In fact, a quick glance around the Giardini or the Arsenale is sufficient to realize that there are many more pigeons than blackbirds. They are less solitary and like flocking around touristic attractions which they litter with their droppings. Italian cities like Venice are their favourite destinations since there is a lot of stuff to feed upon. Despite their wings, they are not as used to fly as they should be. They walk most of the time and they always manage to be in everybody's way. While a form of almost human intelligence springs from the eyes of the blackbirds, the pigeons have an irritating blank stare. They are the power animals of the majority of the Biennale's visitors, those who walk aimlessly around causing commotion where there should be absolute quietness. Certainly the pigeon was the protector of that teenage student that disconnected an installation from its power source in order to use the wall socket to charge the battery of his cellphone. When I saw that, I could not believe my eyes. The only thing I managed to do was to swear. He did not understand why I was in a rage and as I reconnected the installation to the electric system he just said he had thought that his action was a perfectly normal thing to do.

The only positive thing that one can say about the pigeons is that they are not as bad as the seagulls. The latter are fewer in number but much more aggressively brave. They steal food from people's hands, even whole sandwiches. When very hungry they do not disdain killing pigeons; they break their necks, pluck their feathers and eat their entrails (they do not dislike dead rats, but those are promptly disposed of by the personnel of the Biennale, so there are not so many to be found). It seems that they have forgotten of being seabirds. So, although the Biennale is not their natural habitat they show no intention to leave. Their eyes express the hostility that only wild carnivorous animals can have. Their brains and their hearts are far from having been domesticated and although they are accustomed to be near civilized human beings they have lost nothing of their feral nature. The seagull is the power animal of a minority of visitors, but they are so bellicose that a few of them are enough to spread terror like a battalion of storm troopers entering a Polish village during WW2. They do not content themselves with disrespecting the staff of the Biennale or with insulting them (which would be too much anyway). They do not disdain threatening them and even picking fights. Personnel of the weaker sex fare worse than males; since they look more vulnerable they suffer more verbal attacks than their colleagues. Some adult men and teenage bullies like to play macho with a defenceless girl, although most of them immediately become more docile when they are confronted by another male. Others simply go for it. They are ready to turn a quarrel into a physical aggression.

One of the most unpleasant situations in which I got involved happened in 2011, the same year in which I found a turd on the pavilion's floor. It was a rainy day and as usual I had to invite all visitors to leave their umbrellas near the entrance in order to prevent them from dripping water on the floor and, most importantly, from inadvertently damaging the artworks. A tall man came in with his wife and when I asked him to leave his umbrella by the door he refused to do so on the grounds that it was raining outside and he had the right to walk around with it. Moreover, he did not make any effort to simulate politeness and replied in French to my English request. "Il pleut" he kept on saying, "It rains". That was enough to qualify himself as an asshole. If I had been more experienced I would have let him go in anyway, keeping an eye on him in order to intercept the tip of his umbrella had it swung too close to an artwork. Instead I went on urging him to comply with our rules, which he did not have any intention to respect. As a last attempt to stand up for myself I told him that he could only stay in the anteroom of the pavilion but could not cross the threshold of the main room. He acted as if I were invisible, taking no notice of my words and dignity: more assholism. He went into the main room and visited the exhibition, his umbrella dribbling rainwater all along. Luckily he did not damage anything, nonetheless I was literally mad at him. When he was about to go out I told him how uncivilized he had been and that I should have taken a picture of him with my cellphone in order to have the *carabinieri* (one of the many Italian police forces) go after him and throw him out of the Giardini. Obviously I knew that such a thing would never have happened, but I was so infuriated by his lack of respect that I wanted him to know what would have been an appropriate retribution for his attitude. So, I waved my cellphone like a mythological weapon endowed with the power to restore justice for the oppressed. I expected him to keep on ignoring me. Perhaps to insult me, to tell me that I was a born loser with a lousy job. I could never have imagined that his reaction would be a physical assault, that his mute contempt for the little authority I had been invested with would give way to such a rush of brutality as I had never been personally exposed to in any workplace. It was quick but shocking, all the more so because it happened at the Biennale, not on the terrace of a football stadium. The French-speaking man tried to punch me in the face two or three times. I managed to ward off his blows, but if I had been slower he surely would have left quite a bruise on my left cheek. After his unsuccessful attempts at hurting me he decided to leave and I stood where I was, still unable to grasp the magnitude of what had just happened. Only after some further consideration I came to the conclusion that I could not let him get away with what he had done. So, I checked where he was heading to and reported the incident to the *carabinieri* patrolling the Giardini. When he noticed that I was pointing at him he tried to hide inside a nearby pavilion, but dumb as he was he chose one with the walls made of see-through glass panels. The rest of the story is quite predictable: the *carabinieri* caught him, asked him to show his I.D., wrote down all the details they needed to identify him, then came back to me and informed me that I had ninety days' time to take him to court. I thought and still think that he deserved to be sued, but I did not do it because the Italian judiciary system is so clogged with trials and civil actions that I preferred not to contribute to its slowness. I presume that afterwards, not seeing any form of punishment coming his way, that man never gave a second thought to how he had behaved. Probably he still thinks that in Italy one can assault a person who is working without having to pay for it. On my part, I learnt that the art world is not a place nor a state of mind immune from people's worst manners and basest nature.

Suffering an aggression is unpleasant for anybody. But it is certainly more traumatic for someone whose psychological condition is already distressed by a society that marginalizes them because of their gender, religion, skin colour, or ethnicity. That is what happens to many immigrants living in Italy, a country that is oblivious of their existence except when they commit a crime. Usually their voices are suffocated by the Italians' unwillingness to listen to them and they are still considered by many as temporary foreign bodies not entitled to reclaim the full spectrum of the basic human rights. They are powerless and susceptible to being abused like, for instance, the African woman who cleaned the public lavatories in the Giardini who was attacked by an entire family of visitors. She was far from her homeland and paid little money to stick her nose and hands into toilet bowls plastered with the foulest excretions produced by perfect strangers with whom she had nothing in common. Being an immigrant from the Dark Continent hired with a flimsy employment contract to scrub toilets mostly used by white Europeans very likely put her in a rather odd frame of mind. Finding herself in such a condition must have prompted her to notice some similarities between what was happening to her and the stories of old colonial rule she might have read in some book about African history or even heard from the elders who had witnessed history in the making. Of course she was not a slave, but what she earned must have been barely sufficient to make ends meet if she had a family to support and a rent to pay. Probably she was not abused daily as her ancestors had been, but she was certainly not expected to complain aloud about people who locked themselves into the lavatories' cubicles for fifteen minutes and left them as if they had thrown a hand grenade into the toilet bowl. And very often the loos at the Biennale do look like a trench during the battle of the Somme. It could not be otherwise, since every day they are used by hundreds if not thousands of visitors. On the busiest days there are moments when the floor is covered with a sticky blend of water and urine and the wastebaskets overflow with paper and tampons, moments in which they do not look much better than the toilets of a filling station on a heavily trafficked highway. No matter how hard the cleaners mop and scrub, in a few minutes the place is dirty all over again. So it is only natural that they look forward 6pm, when they close the door and tidy up one last time before going home. It is just perfectly normal, too, that at closing time many visitors want to use the toilets before leaving the Giardini. They could buy a coffee in order to use the facilities of Bar Paradiso, just in front of the main exit, but apparently only a few are ready to spend 1.20 euros to have access to them. Or perhaps they dread the petrifying stare of Rem Coca-Koolhaas, who looks at them from a venomously green-toned portrait that hangs right in front of the bar. Either way, they run to the toilets inside the Giardini - especially those between the Belgian and the Duth pavilions, being the nearest ones to the exit - and if they find out that they cannot use them they complain to the cleaners either because their watch reads 5.59pm or because they think that the expensive ticket they purchased gives them unlimited rights over anything and anybody connected with the Biennale. Probably it started like that, with an argument about a door closed five minutes before 6pm or with a presumption of racial superiority, when that African woman was assailed by a Dutch couple and their teenage son and daughter. When she informed the family that she would not let them in the mother jumped on her and a fight between the two women broke out. In a few seconds the entire family was possessed by the spirits of their Boer forefathers who more than one century before had to fight tooth and nail to secure a tiny plot of South African land. All of a sudden that woman reminded them of how hard their long dead compatriots had to struggle to survive in the Dark Continent. They resumed the ferocity with which the Boers slaughtered the natives whose land they wanted to rob and in the heat of the moment all four of them attacked the woman like a pack of boerboels. Eventually some other people intervened and stopped the fight, but not before the cleaning lady bit the son in an attempt to free herself from the grip of her assailants. An action that led her attackers to add a last touch of racist drama to what had just happened. In fact, they said that odds were that she was HIV positive and that the boy might have been infected by her. They demanded to be taken to the hospital to have him checked by a doctor. I do not know how the story ended, since I was not an eyewitness and heard about it only the following day. I presume that if eventually they went to the hospital some nurse poured some disinfectant on the boy's wound and that he is still alive. As regards the African woman, I do not remember of having seen her around much after that incident. Perhaps the way she reacted made her lose her employment or be assigned to work in another place. What I have no doubt about is that because of her humble job and the colour of her skin she surely did not manage to make her voice heard as much as that of the Dutch family.

Some people are knowledgeable in art but they visit the Biennale looking for the wrong thing. And they never lose a chance to utter their dissatisfaction. I had to listen to the complaints of people who were disappointed because they could not find any exhibition of baroque art or because in what they saw they could not discern the same grace of the paintings by Tiepolo and Tintoretto. Other visitors think that the Architecture Biennale is a trade fair and attend it with the idea that the various pavilions are a sort of pharaonic booths displaying innovative ideas and new materials to build houses for the perfect bourgeois family. So, although sometimes they can come upon what they look for, a number of professionals spend most of their visit walking among exhibits which they deem not only uninteresting but even detrimental to the advancement of architecture. Having a pragmatic frame of mind they do not manage to understand why they are offered theories and solutions that sound like science-fiction or pure utopia. They want to be presented with suggestions that can help them solve the housing problems of real people living in the real world. They could not care less about the thermal insulation of a Mongolian yurt or a wall made with bacteria that change their colour with light modulation and other indoor conditions. At best they can be amused, but surely not thrilled or seriously captivated by something that they can not immediately put into practice. For them architecture has to do with erecting buildings for clients who, especially if they live in culturally depressed areas such as the mainland West of Venice called Pianura Padana, do not want to live in a house that might be too conspicuous in their neighbourhood. Better stick to the traditional, unchallenging design of a home sweet home à la Simpsons. Both architects and clients of this mindset want to save money and time whilst retaining a taste for banality which guarantees that in the future they will never have to blame themselves for having been too daring. They want to be inspired by inventive carpenters and bricklayers. They can not be bothered with the wishful thinking and the flights of fancy of young architects who have never set foot in a construction site and could not tell mortar from custard. They are far less concerned with saving the environment than with feeling safe within their comfort zone. If they can not be given something they can work with in the short term, they prefer to look at the good old plywood models of famous buildings or at the shiny plastic ones of airports and concert halls.

People can be disappointed for a variety of reasons, some of which depend on the inefficiency of the personnel of the Biennale while some others depend upon the visitors' own cultural deficiencies and modest rational faculties. Nothing new under the sun, if one is to believe the story that back in 1959 the visitors of the Paul Gauguin exhibition held at the Chicago Art Institute complained that the colours of the paintings were not as brilliant as those of the reproductions they had seen in postcards and magazines. Nowadays the food served at the bars of the Biennale would put anybody on solid ground to complain. Not simply because its price is disproportionate to its quality and quantity - a ludicrously small portion of vegetarian couscous, not much bigger than a billiard ball, served in a plastic box costs around 9 euros - but also because it is often served by bartenders whose carelessness is made more conspicuous by their nonexistent command of English. Expressions of verbal courtesy like "please", "thank you", "you are welcome", or "would you like" rarely pepper their conversations with their customers. Words are usually kept at a bare minimum, so their manners often have a brusque edge that some people can find rather out of line. However, what many complains are about is the Biennale itself. In fact, since it requires a little degree of general knowledge and concentration, a considerable number of visitors do not manage to enjoy it. Having little cognizance of the history of art and of the current practices in contemporary art, they do not have the proper intellectual tools to grasp the artworks' meaning (when there is one) or to understand how they were assembled. That is not a crime: anybody has the right to visit an exhibition even if they are not experts on the subject (I do it regularly myself). But unfortunately a lot of people do not seem to be aware of their cultural limits and personal biases. The idea that their inability to connect with what is in front of their eyes might be due to their lack of preparation never pops up in their mind. They always think it is the artist's fault. He or she is guilty of having made something which does not meet their expectations. And what many of them look for is pure entARTainment, some cheap fun that they can post on Facebook and Instagram. When they talk about contemporary art they think about Maurizio Cattelan, Damien Hirst, Takashi Murakami, Banksy. Their drive is a need of visual stimuli that they expect to appease with a parade of artworks which, instead of challenging their imagination, can stir their childlike sense of wonderment. Individuals who are not gifted with any psychological depth, those who live on the surface of their own existence, assume - one might suspect that they even demand - that everything they set their eyes on is self-explanatory, flat, capable of being effortlessly experienced and made sense of by means of the same critical thinking they deploy when in front of their telly or of their tablet. They look for the unseen but do not want to focus their attention on the unknown. Perhaps they must not be blamed for that, for they just behave as is dictated by human nature. It is explained in one of the classic texts of 20th Century scientific research. In "The Naked Ape" Desmond Morris wrote that "in all exploratory behaviour, whether artistic or scientific, there is the ever-present battle between the neophilic and neophobic urges. The former drives us on to new experiences, makes us crave for novelty. The latter holds us back, makes us take refuge in the familiar. We are constantly in a state of shifting balance between the conflicting attractions of the exciting new stimulus and the friendly old one. If we lost our neophilia we would stagnate. If we lost our neophobia, we would rush headlong into disaster. This state of conflict does not merely account for the more obvious fluctuations in fashions and fads, in hair-styles and clothing, in furniture and cars; it is also the very basis of our whole cultural progression. We explore and we retrench, we investigate and we stabilize. Step by step we expand our awareness and understanding both of ourselves and of the complex environment we live in"[12]. The real problem is that too many people know too little and do not seem willing to widen the scope of their knowledge, thus becoming unable to perform the act of mental breathing described by Morris. They live a life of cultural apnea and therefore anything they see at the Biennale must appeal to their sense of humour or kindle their pleasure at being stupefied by the things that toy with what they are already well acquainted with. That is why this particular typology of visitors go for big dimensions, cartoonish installations, bright colours, references to popular culture and the entertainment industry. The adjectives they use to describe what they like are "cool", "amazing", "awesome", "great". The same words they would use to talk about a pair of sneakers or their latest Instagram idol. The works of Jeff Koons and Andy Warhol are still topical for them, albeit only for their visual impact and for their obvious power to amuse their beholders. Many people benefit from the democratization of culture, but for them this does not mean having the possibility of accessing art but rather the expectation that contemporary art should conform to the current trends in the entertainment industry. Thus, attending an exhibition becomes a pursuit of pure fun and what used to be a noble, enlightening activity is now just one more way to spend a Sunday afternoon with one's brain switched off. So, it looks like that "the social practices of one generation tend to get codified into the 'game' of the next. Finally, the game is passed on as a joke, like a skeleton stripped of its flesh"[13] and it becomes clear that it is still necessary to democratise culture "but that also has its risks, if that means that we make ideas banal in order to make them accessible to everyone. That is not democratising culture, but rather corrupting it and replacing it with a caricature. The democratisation of culture can only be understood as the creation of conditions that facilitate and promote access to culture for those who are prepared to make the necessary intellectual effort to enjoy and enhance their lives through culture"[14]. An issue that the most conscientious artists feel compelled to tackle, since they can not pretend not to know that "the extension of the base of participants in the cultural life of the community presents its own questions. What is clear is that this end must be achieved by increasing the number of those who, through opportunity, can appreciate and contribute to culture on its most exalted plane, rather than lowering the level of culture to the equipment of all"[15]. Indeed what happens at the Biennale is not exactly what worried Mark Rothko: the level of culture is not lowered to the equipment of all even if the number of attendants keeps on rising. For most artists and curators exhibit artworks that do not make concessions to the visitors, but the real problem is that nobody seems to care if the latter understand the meaning of an installation or the narrative of a video. If people go home after one day at the Biennale feeling better, enlightened, with a different perspective on the world, willing to attend exhibitions more regularly, feeling more responsive to the artworks, looking in a different way at the objects and images which are around them. Nobody wonders about all this because nowadays an art exhibition is not judged for how it affects the public but rather for how many tickets are sold and how many bodies cross the threshold of a museum regardless of the reaction of the brains inside them. In "The Society of the Spectacle" Guy Debord noted that after the primitive stage of capitalist accumulation workers became consumers whose leisure time was as valuable as their labour power because they could partake of (i.e. spend their money to buy) an abundance of commodities. This led to a society in which everybody is both a producer and a consumer all the time, a society in which working hours and leisure time overlap and often become indistinguishable from each other. A world in which also when one thinks to be idle he or she is nonetheless either producing or consuming something, be it a physical object or something intangible such as a story, an exhibition, a movie, personal information. At the office or at the Biennale, in a factory or in a luxury resort in the middle of the ocean, one is constantly producing, buying, or sharing objects sold in the retail market, providing big data stored in someone else's machines, creating Facebook and Instagram contents which in turn produce feelings, aspirations, discontents, empathy, sense of belonging. It goes on all over the world without pause and everyone is doing their part. So much so that Jonathan Crary has theorized that the only true revolutionary act to counter such society is to sleep, because "in its profound uselessness and intrinsic passivity, with the incalculable losses it causes in production time, circulation, and consumption, sleep will always collide with the demands of a 24/7 universe. The huge portion of our lives that we spend asleep, freed from a morass of simulated needs, subsists as one of the great human affronts to the voraciousness of contemporary capitalism. Sleep is an uncompromising interruption of the theft of time from us by capitalism. Most of the seemingly irreducible necessities of human life - hunger, thirst, sexual desire, and recently the need for friendship - have been remade into commodified or financialized forms. Sleep poses the idea of a human need and interval of time that cannot be colonized and harnessed to a massive engine of profitability, and thus remains an incongruous anomaly and site of crisis in the global present. In spite of all the scientific research in this area, it frustrates and confounds any strategies to exploit or foreshape it. The stunning, inconceivable reality is that nothing of value can be extracted from it"[16]. So, whenever one is awake, he or she is producing or consuming something. It is clear that the Biennale's attendees consume the Biennale, but what exactly do they produce? The answer is simple: they produce the Biennale itself. In fact, any exhibition could not exist without its visitors, since any art show is curated and mounted to be seen and talked about. Obviously theirs is not an act of artistic or intellectual creation, but much more an operation of spatial consolidation. They fill in the Giardini and the Arsenale with their bodies, they occupy spaces in the internet and the social networks with millions of pictures, tweets, posts, videos, comments, reviews that help the Biennale be omnipresent. They buy tote bags, t-shirts, and badges that spread its brand everywhere. When they purchase their ticket they make it look as successful as the latest Marvel movie: with the volume of the data they produce about the Biennale they assist it in overwhelming other art events and all information which might dare differ from the official narrative. As has been pointed out by Boris Groys, it is in the very nature of contemporary art to exist as a series of "artistic events, performances, temporary exhibitions that demonstrate the transitory character of the present order of things and the rules that govern contemporary social behaviour"[17]. Such a state of impermanence, in which the objects that used to be called artworks are less important than the event that hosts them and the image it projects on society, is made explicit at the

Biennale, where the emphasis is put on the typically capitalistic drive towards unlimited growth (more visitors, more pavilions, more opening days) rather than on what significance the exhibits will have for the future generations, what legacy they will leave behind after the show ends in November. It is true that art happenings were a common practice in the 60's and the 70's, and that even "the artists of Futurism and Dada produced artistic events revealing the decay and obsoleteness of the present. But the production of art events is even more characteristic of contemporary art, with its culture of performance and participation. Today's artistic events cannot be preserved and contemplated like traditional artworks. However, they can be documented, 'covered', narrated and commented on. Traditional art produced art objects. Contemporary art produces information about art events"[18]. The Biennale is transitory, though recurring, and can hardly leave a trail when it ends, because it is mostly made up of installations that are doomed to be disassembled and the few enduring artworks that are exhibited there are destined to be incohesively dispersed here and there in private collections and public museums. It is not surprising that it must live off its own narrative, and consequently it needs people who read it, help write it, and above all accept it unquestioningly.

In the first series of his "Museum Photographs" Thomas Struth included a picture he shot in 1992 inside the Gallerie dell'Accademia in Venice. In that image (as in those taken at the Louvre, at the National Gallery in London, and in many other renowned museums) a quiet group of some twenty visitors appear to be watching the artworks in complete silence, as if they did not want to intrude on the banquet depicted in Paolo Veronese's "The Feast in the House of Levi", the painting that the German photographer used as a backdrop for his shot. A few people are blurred, caught by the long exposure of the picture while they move about like diaphanous ghosts. The other characters are perfectly still, focused on the masterpieces of the Venetian School of the 16th Century. The overall impression is of an orderly group of people visiting the gallery without uttering so much as a whisper. Probably it was not exactly like that and Struth managed to record an ideal, almost abstract situation instead of the actual conditions of that room in that particular moment. Very likely one could hear a number of sounds of human and artificial nature and, on top of that, smell sweat, food, cheap aftershave, stale cigarette smoke, expensive perfume and many more scents and stinks. Photography can record only what is perceived by the eye. However, it often produces images that tell much more than what is captured on film or on a mosaic of pixels. As is probably the case with Struth's photograph, sometimes an image communicates ideas and inspires feelings which bear little relation to reality. Especially if it plays upon old preconceptions which can still influence the observer during his or her reading of it. For instance the assumption - taken for granted by many people even nowadays - that the majority of the visitors of museums and art galleries are extremely refined individuals who have a paralyzing mystical experience whenever they are near an artwork. In my opinion Struth's image is somewhat deceiving inasmuch as it conveys a sensation of quietness which unfortunately is seldom experienced at an art exhibition attended by the general public. It prompts one to think that the power animal of most museum goers is the blackbird, while in fact the pigeon seems to qualify as their totem animal. Therefore, I would not take the photograph of the Gallerie dell'Accademia as an appropriate counterpart of an ordinary day at the Biennale, since the quietness it depicts can seldom be enjoyed for more than ten minutes. Instead, I would look at Arthur Fellig's shots if I had to find a truly representative photograph of the Biennale's visitors. Between the 1930's and the 1940's Fellig, better known as Weegee, worked in New York for popular tabloids. He provided them with shots of crime scenes, corpses, mobsters in handcuffs, car crashes, street fights, pavements splattered with blood, buildings on fire, freaks, prostitutes, drunkards, all the accidents that happened in the city at night and all the nocturnal animals which, merely because of their own existence, could stir a feeling of horrified attraction in those who browsed the "New York Post" or the "Herald Tribune" looking for a reassurance of their own respectability. He was always the first reporter to reach the scene of a crime and very often he managed to be there even ahead of the police. Usually he found a crowd of people crammed around the victim of a stabbing or gaping at a building enveloped by flames. Men, women, and children flocked around a crime scene or an urban disaster in order to inject a dose of excitement in their dull lives. They were there to enjoy the show, to be entertained by a Grand Guignol that Hollywood movies dared not offer them and whose gruesome details they could not read in the pages of their hard-boiled novels.

Looking at those people Weegee had the intuition that they were a real and proper sideshow that was worth photographing. So, he took pictures of them while they struggled to have a better view of a scene which they probably could not make any sense of. Very likely they did not have any idea of what caused the drama that was unfolding before their eyes, but blood, screams, whining sirens, ambulances, flashing lights, fire created a magnetic field capable of kindling and attracting their dormant curiosity. Every big or small tragedy dragged them out of their flat existences with the promise of a thrilling spectacle. Yet, unbeknownst to them, Weegee realized that they were the real carnival, anonymous performers of a freak show which, although far less shocking than the traditional ones, was nonetheless puzzling and surely interesting in terms of anthropological and social studies. In fact, they were not dissimilar from the ancient Romans who amused themselves with the bloodbaths held in the Colosseum. But there was also an undisputable analogy between them and those people who throughout history had gathered in city squares to watch a public decapitation or the burning of a witch, that is to say those people who had transformed a dreadful scene such as the death of a human being into a form of mass entertainment. It did not matter whether a tragic occasion was accidental or planned and organized by the authorities, if it was the result of a crime or the administering of justice: in Weegee's pictures the New Yorkers gawking at a corpse on a sidewalk had the same facial expressions of the fans of Hollywood celebrities catching a glimpse of their idols on the red carpet. The entertainment industry provided them with cheap excitement and diversion through movies, radio dramas, comics, and pulp magazines, but apparently they were unable to draw a line between a murder in a detective story and a real dead man lying facedown on the street. Paving the way for Guy Debord, they foreshadowed a society in which everything is liable to be turned into a spectacle and experienced as a form of entertainment. In such a world everybody can no longer distinguish reality from fiction, individuals from characters, war footage from a video game, demanding cultural activities from carefree leisure, an art exhibition like the Biennale from an amusement park. People become unable to contextualize and assess the value of what they see and consequently their expectations and reactions are in no way affected by the shift from one object of observation to another or from one environment to another. That is why they do not understand for what reason they are supposed to treat an oil painting with much more consideration than a postcard and why their attitude inside a museum can not be the same as the one they have in a shopping mall. For those who equate all recreational activities with pure and simple entertainment anything - a book, an art exhibition, an archaeological site, a wildlife sanctuary, an historical city like Venice - must lend itself to being bought and consumed like a product whose ultimate purpose is to offer them some fun. What they seek is light, carefree entertainment. In this respect, exhibition-going seems to have suffered the same decadence that from the middle of the 19th Century turned exploratory travelling into tourism. "Formerly travel required long planning, large expense, and great investments of time. It involved risks to health or even to life. The traveler was active. Now he became passive. Instead of an athletic exercise, travel became a spectator sport. This change can be described in a word. It was the decline of the traveler and the rise of the tourist. There is a wonderful, but neglected, precision in these words. The old English noun 'travel' (in the sense of a journey) was originally the same word as 'travail' (meaning 'trouble', 'work', or 'torment'). And the word 'travail', in turn, seems to have been derived, through the French, from a popular Latin or Common Romanic word *trepalium*, which meant a three-staked instrument of torture. To journey - to 'travail', or (later) to travel - then was to do something laborious or troublesome. The traveler was an active man at work. In the early nineteenth century a new word came into the English language which gave a clue to the changed character of world travel, especially from the American point of view. This was the word 'tourist' - at first hyphenated as 'tour-ist'. Our American dictionary now defines a tourist as "a person who makes a pleasure trip" or "a person who makes a tour, especially for pleasure". Significantly, too, the word 'tour' in 'tourist' was derived by back-formation from the Latin *tornus*, which in turn came from the Greek word for a tool describing a circle. The traveler, then, was working at something; the tourist was a pleasure-seeker. The traveler was active; he went strenuously in search of people, of adventure, of experience. The tourist is passive; he expects interesting things to happen to him. He goes 'sight-seeing' (a word, by the way, which came in about the same time, with its first use recorded in 1847). He expects everything to be done to him and for him"[19]. The difference between the old traveler and the modern tourist described by Daniel J. Boorstin over half a century ago seems to be exactly the same as that between the old-time exhibition-goers and those of today. While the former searched for an enriching, almost spiritual experience the latter look for fun and amusement. And where could this be more evident than at Venice Biennale, the oldest and most famous contemporary art circus held in a city that has become one big touristic attraction? Where could the society of the spectacle be most resplendent if not in a theme park located inside another theme park?

Afterword

This book was written piecemeal in the course of about seven years, during which President Paolo Baratta was replaced by President Roberto Cicutto and Venetians, much to my surprise, chose to re-elect Luigi Brugnaro as city mayor. Its writing was slowed down and often disrupted by some accidents that happen in everybody's life, particularly the death of my father (following that of my mother) and the end of a very special relationship. For long periods of time I did not have the energy nor the right moments to work on it. Moreover, since English is not my mother tongue I had to struggle with words and punctuation, rediscovering a language that I am used to read but not to write at length. Therefore, in this book there are some shifts in style, irregularities, mood changes, perhaps some sharp corners due to the constant updates. It also contains many quotations, and to explain why they are there and how they relate to what is purely mine I can not but add a further one: "the text contains large chunks of quotation, both to give a flavour of the material being discussed - and to save time and effort on the part of the author. It should be understood that these quotations are being used to illustrate a specific argument and that to

Afterword

keep the text as brief as possible the author does not fully explore the contradictions or assumptions that any given quotation may contain"[1]. After all, as they say, nothing is really new in contemporary art. What matters is that everything in this book is true, it happened to me or to my colleagues and friends, it was experienced by people of all ages and levels of education. It is how Venice Biennale and the city itself function. It is what very probably will never be written by those who have the power of speech. It is the rest of the story.

Acknowledgments

It would take too many pages to thank all the people whom I met at the Biennale, those who trusted me with their artworks, curatorial projects, and valuable premises. But surely I want to express my thanks to B.D.B., P.V.C., D.S., E.W., D.B., A.V., R., J.D.V., I.V., F.D. K.G., V.M., E.B., J.B., P.B. & O.M., T.G. & K.A., M.V., A.-C.S., J.D.G. & H.T., T., R.L.G., A.C., S.M.B., B.D., J.W., C.G., K.L., S.V.P., E.V., N.G., S.G., J.C., P.V., C.G., S.D.C. A.D.B., P.M.. My apologies to all the people whom I forgot to mention.

I also want to thank all the light technicians, decorators, electricians, photographers, graphic designers, exhibition managers, assistants to the artists and curators, architects, employees of the cleaning companies, carpenters, workingmen that I have worked with. Too many to mention by name but all of them necessary to run the show.

Thanks to my colleagues at the Biennale who willingly helped me and to all my friends who substituted for me when I needed a day off. They know who they are.

I am indebted to N.Z. for bequeathing to me his job at the Biennale; definitely not the job of my life but at least a way to make ends meet. I am equally thankful towards C.F.-C. for having helped me get a regular employment

Acknowledgments

contract when that seemed beyond hope.

I am grateful to D.T., who encouraged me to pick English when I had to choose what subject to study at the university, and to R.C., who one day told me "Write a book!".

My warmest thanks go to C.F.G. For the good times.

Notes

Chapter 1

1 Mario Vargas Llosa, "The Heart of Darkness" in "Touchstones. Essays on Literature, Art, and Politics", Farrar, Straus and Giroux, 2011.
2 Aldous Huxley, "The Divine Within. Selected Writings on Enlightenment", Harper Perennial Modern Classics, 2013.
3 Charles Bukowski, "The Genius of the Crowd" in "The Pleasures of the Damned. Poems, 1951-1983", Harper Collins, 2007.
4 Aldous Huxley, "The Divine Within. Selected Writings on Enlightenment", Harper Perennial Modern Classics, 2013.
5 Mark Rothko, "The Artist's Reality. Philosophies of Art", Yale University Press, 2004.
6 Salvatore Settis, "Italia S.p.A. L'Assalto al Patrimonio Culturale", Einaudi, 2002. My translation. Here is the original excerpt in Italian: "Proprio nel nostro Paese si è elaborata negli ultimi secoli una cultura della conservazione molto attenta e molto sofisticata, che ha valorizzato i singoli monumenti, grandi e piccoli, come parte di un insieme incardinato nel territorio, di una rete ricca di significati identitari, nella quale il valore di ogni singolo monumento od oggetto d'arte risulta non dal suo isolamento, ma dal suo innestarsi in un vitale contesto. È questa cultura che ha in primo luogo garantito in Italia la conservazione dei monumenti in misura maggiore che altrove; e che, fatto capitale, ha consentito di percepire e codificare il significato anche dei monumenti «minori», valorizzandolo mediante

il riferimento al loro contesto di origine, la fitta trama dei rapporti con altri monumenti, minori e maggiori, che si spiegano e si illuminano a vicenda".

7 Ibid. My translation. Here is the original excerpt in Italian: "Quello che costituisce la nostra identità, la rete che ci avvolge e che ci identifica, è che il nostro patrimonio culturale sono le città nelle quali viviamo, le chiese in cui entriamo, le case e i palazzi in cui abitiamo o che visitiamo, le nostre coste e le nostre montagne. Il nostro patrimonio culturale non è un'entità estranea, calata da fuori, ma qualcosa che abbiamo creato nel tempo e con cui abbiamo convissuto per generazioni e generazioni, per secoli e secoli; non un gruzzolo nel salvadanaio, da spendere se occorre, ma la nostra memoria, la nostra anima".

8 Michel de Montaigne, "On Habit: And on Never Easily Changing a Traditional Law", in "The Complete Essays", Penguin, 2003.

9 John Ruskin, "The Stones of Venice", Da Capo Press, 2003.

10 Salvatore Settis, "Italia S.p.A. L'Assalto al Patrimonio Culturale", Einaudi, 2002. My translation. Here is the original excerpt in Italian: "Oggi l'eredità culturale dell'Italia è degradata a mero valore economico, a una risorsa di cui ci si può disfare a piacimento. Ma non c'è nulla che dia la misura dello stato di salute di una società quanto il rapporto che essa riesce ad avere coi propri monumenti e col proprio paesaggio".

11 John Berger, "Selected Essays", Vintage, 2001.

12 Slavoj Zizek, "Event: A Philosophical Journey Through a Concept", Melville House, 2014.

13 Aldous Huxley, "The Divine Within. Selected Writings on Enlightenment", Harper Perennial Modern Classics, 2013.

Chapter 2

1 Michel de Montaigne, "On Prognostications", in "The Complete

Essays", Penguin, 2003.
2 Junichiro Tanizaki, "In Praise of Shadows", Leete's Island Books, 1977.
3 Henry James, "The Aspern Papers", in "The Turn of the Screw and Other Novels", Signet Classics, 2007.
4 Tiziano Scarpa "Venice Is a Fish. A Cultural Guide", Serpent's Tail, 2009.
5 Jeoff Dyer, "Sacked", in "Working the Room", Canongate, 2011.
6 Emil Cioran, "A Short History of Decay", Skyhorse Publishing, 2012.
7 Ibid.
8 Marshall McLuhan, "Understanding Media. The Extensions of Man", Gingko Press, 2013.
9 Mario Vargas Llosa, "The Thief in the Empty House" in "Touchstones. Essays on Literature, Art, and Politics", Farrar, Straus and Giroux, 2011.
10 T.S. Eliot, "Murder in the Cathedral", Part 1, in "The Complete Poems and Plays", Faber & Faber, 1969.
11 Emil Cioran, "A Short History of Decay", Skyhorse Publishing, 2012.
12 Philip Larkin, "The Dedicated", in "Collected Poems", The Marvell Press and Faber & Faber, 1988.
13 William Shakespeare, "Macbeth", Act 1, Scene 5, in "The Complete Works" edited by John Jowett et al., Oxford University Press, 2005.
14 Hans Ulrich Obrist, "Ways of Curating", Penguin, 2015.
15 Mikhail Yurevich Lermontov, "A Hero of Our Time", Penguin Classics, 1979.

Chapter 3

1 Lina Bo Bardi, "Window Displays" in "Stones Against Diamonds", AA Publications, 2013.
2 Ibid.

Notes

3 Lord George Gordon Byron, "Ode on Venice", in "Complete Works", Delphi Classics, 2012.
4 Guy Debord, "The Society of the Spectacle", Rebel Press, 1983.
5 Neil Postman, "Amusing Ourselves to Death. Public Discourse in the Age of Show Business", Penguin, 2005.
6 Ibid.
7 Aaron James, "Assholes. A theory", Doubleday, 2012.
8 Ibid.
9 Richard Laing, "The Divided Self", Penguin Classics, 2010.
10 Jack Lemmon as Mel Edison in "The Prisoner of Second Avenue", Warner Bros. Pictures, 1975.
11 Richard Laing, "The Divided Self", Penguin Classics, 2010.
12 Desmond Morris, "The Naked Ape. A Zoologist's Study of the Human Animal", Delta, 1967.
13 Marshall McLuhan, "Understanding Media. The Extensions of Man", Gingko Press, 2013.
14 Mario Vargas Llosa, "Culture and the New International Order" in "Touchstones. Essays on Literature, Art, and Politics", Farrar, Straus and Giroux, 2011.
15 Mark Rothko, "The Artist's Reality. Philosophies of Art", Yale University Press, 2004.
16 Jonathan Crary, "24/7. Late Capitalism and the Ends of Sleep", Verso, 2013.
17 Boris Groys, "In the Flow", Verso Books, 2016.
18 Ibid.
19 Daniel J. Boorstin, "The Image. A Guide to Pseudo-Events in America", Vintage Books, 2012.

Afterword

1 Stewart Home, "The Assault on Culture. Utopian Currents from Lettrisme to Class War", Aporia Press and Unpopular Books, 1988.

www.ingramcontent.com/pod-product-compliance
Lightning Source LLC
Chambersburg PA
CBHW020646220526
45464CB00001B/308